LINDSEY FERRENTINO

Lindsey Ferrentino is an American playwright. Her plays include *Ugly Lies the Bone* (Lyttelton Theatre at the National Theatre, London; Roundabout Theatre Company, New York; with over one hundred productions worldwide), *Amy and the Orphans* (Roundabout Theatre Company), *This Flat Earth* (Playwrights Horizons), *The Year to Come* (La Jolla Playhouse), *The Artist* (co-adapted with Drew McOnie; Theatre Royal Plymouth), the book for Broadway-bound musical *The Queen of Versailles* (with music and lyrics by Stephen Schwartz, starring Kristin Chenoweth and F. Murray Abraham, The Colonial Theater), and *The Fear of 13* (starring Adrien Brody, at the Donmar Warehouse, London). Her plays have been translated into Spanish, German and Portuguese and have been produced across the US, in London, Germany, Spain and Venezuela.

She is directing her first feature film: an adaptation of her play *Amy and the Orphans* for Jason Bateman's Aggregate Films, in addition to various film and TV projects at Netflix and Sony Pictures. She is the recipient of The Arc's prize for Entertainment Industry Excellence for her writing centered on disability inclusion. Other prizes include the Kesserling, ASCAP Cole Porter Playwriting Prize, Paul Newman Drama Award, Laurents/Hatcher Award, NYU Distinguished Alumna Award, and Hunter College's 40 Under 40 Distinguished Alumna. BFA: NYU. MFA: Hunter College and The Yale School of Drama.

Other Titles in this Series

Annie Baker
THE ANTIPODES
THE FLICK
INFINITE LIFE
JOHN

Chris Bush
THE ASSASSINATION OF KATIE HOPKINS
THE CHANGING ROOM
CHRIS BUSH PLAYS: ONE
A DOLL'S HOUSE *after* Ibsen
A DREAM
FAUSTUS: THAT DAMNED WOMAN
HUNGRY
JANE EYRE *after* Brontë
THE LAST NOËL
ROCK/PAPER/SCISSORS
STANDING AT THE SKY'S EDGE
  with Richard Hawley
STEEL

Jez Butterworth
THE FERRYMAN
THE HILLS OF CALIFORNIA
JERUSALEM
JEZ BUTTERWORTH PLAYS: ONE
JEZ BUTTERWORTH PLAYS: TWO
MOJO
THE NIGHT HERON
PARLOUR SONG
THE RIVER
THE WINTERLING

Caryl Churchill
BLUE HEART
CHURCHILL PLAYS: THREE
CHURCHILL PLAYS: FOUR
CHURCHILL PLAYS: FIVE
CHURCHILL: SHORTS
CLOUD NINE
DING DONG THE WICKED
A DREAM PLAY *after* Strindberg
DRUNK ENOUGH TO SAY I LOVE YOU?
ESCAPED ALONE
FAR AWAY
GLASS. KILL. BLUEBEARD'S FRIENDS. IMP.
HERE WE GO
HOTEL
ICECREAM
LIGHT SHINING IN BUCKINGHAMSHIRE
LOVE AND INFORMATION
MAD FOREST
A NUMBER
PIGS AND DOGS
SEVEN JEWISH CHILDREN
THE SKRIKER
THIS IS A CHAIR
THYESTES *after* Seneca
TRAPS
WHAT IF IF ONLY

Lindsey Ferrentino
UGLY LIES THE BONE

Jeremy O. Harris
'DADDY': A MELODRAMA
SLAVE PLAY

Sam Holcroft
COCKROACH
DANCING BEARS
EDGAR & ANNABEL
A MIRROR
PINK
RULES FOR LIVING
THE WARDROBE
WHILE YOU LIE

Branden Jacobs-Jenkins
APPROPRIATE
THE COMEUPPANCE
GLORIA
AN OCTOROON

Lucy Kirkwood
BEAUTY AND THE BEAST
  with Katie Mitchell
BLOODY WIMMIN
THE CHILDREN
CHIMERICA
HEDDA *after* Ibsen
THE HUMAN BODY
IT FELT EMPTY WHEN THE HEART
  WENT AT FIRST BUT IT IS
  ALRIGHT NOW
LUCY KIRKWOOD PLAYS: ONE
MOSQUITOES
NSFW
RAPTURE
SMALL HOURS
TINDERBOX
THE WELKIN

Tony Kushner
ANGELS IN AMERICA –
  PARTS ONE AND TWO
CAROLINE, OR CHANGE
HOMEBODY/KABUL
THE VISIT, OR THE OLD LADY
  COMES TO CALL
  after Friedrich Dürrenmatt

Kimber Lee
UNTITLED F*CK M*SS S**GON PLAY

Bruce Norris
CLYBOURNE PARK
DOWNSTATE
THE LOW ROAD
THE PAIN AND THE ITCH
PURPLE HEART

Lynn Nottage
CLYDE'S
CRUMBS FROM THE TABLE OF JOY
INTIMATE APPAREL
MLIMA'S TALE
RUINED
SWEAT

Jack Thorne
2ND MAY 1997
AFTER LIFE *after* Hirokazu Kore-eda
BUNNY
BURYING YOUR BROTHER IN
  THE PAVEMENT
A CHRISTMAS CAROL *after* Dickens
THE END OF HISTORY…
HOPE
JACK THORNE PLAYS: ONE
JACK THORNE PLAYS: TWO
JUNKYARD
LET THE RIGHT ONE IN
  after John Ajvide Lindqvist
THE MOTIVE AND THE CUE
MYDIDAE
THE SOLID LIFE OF SUGAR WATER
STACY & FANNY AND FAGGOT
WHEN WINSTON WENT TO WAR WITH
  THE WIRELESS
WHEN YOU CURE ME
WOYZECK *after* Büchner

debbie tucker green
BORN BAD
DEBBIE TUCKER GREEN PLAYS: ONE
DIRTY BUTTERFLY
EAR FOR EYE
HANG
NUT
A PROFOUNDLY AFFECTIONATE,
  PASSIONATE DEVOTION TO
  SOMEONE (– *NOUN*)
RANDOM
STONING MARY
TRADE & GENERATIONS
TRUTH AND RECONCILIATION

Lindsey Ferrentino

THE FEAR OF 13

*An original play based on the documentary
of the same title by David Sington*

NICK HERN BOOKS
London
www.nickhernbooks.co.uk

A Nick Hern Book

The Fear of 13 first published as a paperback original in Great Britain in 2024 by Nick Hern Books Limited, The Glasshouse, 49a Goldhawk Road, London W12 8QP

The Fear of 13 copyright © 2024 Lindsey Ferrentino

Lindsey Ferrentino has asserted her right to be identified as the author of this work

Cover image: photograph of Adrien Brody by Billy Kidd; artwork by AKA

Designed and typeset by Nick Hern Books, London
Printed in Great Britain by Mimeo Ltd, Huntingdon, Cambridgeshire PE29 6XX

A CIP catalogue record for this book is available from the British Library

ISBN 978 1 83904 396 3

CAUTION All rights whatsoever in this play are strictly reserved. Requests to reproduce the text in whole or in part should be addressed to the publisher.

Applications for performance, including readings and excerpts, throughout the world should be addressed to Creative Artists Agency, 405 Lexington Avenue, 19th Floor, New York, NY 10174, USA, *tel* 212-556-5675, *email* ally.shuster@caa.com

No performance of any kind may be given unless a licence has been obtained. Applications should be made before rehearsals begin. Publication of this play does not necessarily indicate its availability for performance.

www.nickhernbooks.co.uk/environmental-policy

The Fear of 13 was first performed at the Donmar Warehouse, London, on 4 October 2024, with the following cast:

NICK YARRIS (MAN 1)	Adrien Brody
JACKIE SCHAFFER	Nana Mensah
GUARD	Aidan Kelly
MAN 2/LIEUTENANT WALKER/ SHERIFF 1/NICK'S FATHER/ POLICE OFFICER 2/CAPTAIN/ BAILIFF/ARTHUR CRAIG/ JURY FOREMAN	Ferdy Roberts
MAN 3/JOE BULLEN/WAITER/ PAWN-SHOP OWNER/ OFFICER BENJAMIN WRIGHT	Michael Fox
MAN 4/WESLEY/SHERIFF 2/ CLOAKROOM ATTENDANT/ EDDIE/PUBLIC DEFENDER	Posi Morakinyo
MAN 5/BUTCH/ANTHONY MANILLA/JIMMY BRISBOIS/ PROSECUTOR/CLERK/ OLDER MAN	Tommy Sim'aan
MAN 6/SOME GUARD/ NICK'S MOTHER/ POLICE OFFICER 1/COP/ JUDGE KELLY/JUDGE GILES	Cyril Nri
COVER NICK YARRIS (MAN 1)	Matt McClure
Director	Justin Martin
Set Designer	Miriam Buether
Costume Designer	Brigitte Reiffenstuel
Lighting Designer	Jon Clark
Sound Designer	Ian Dickinson for Autograph
Video Designer	Ash J Woodward
Composer and Music Director	DJ Walde
Wigs, Hair and Make-up Designer	Campbell Young Associates
Casting Director	Anna Cooper CDG
Associate Director	Ed Burnside
Resident Assistant Director	Grace Duggan
Associate Set Designer	Luke Smith

Intimacy Director	Lucy Hind
Fight Directors	Kev McCurdy
	& Sam Lyon-Behan
Voice Coach	Barbara Houseman
Dialect Coach	Aundrea Fudge
Production Manager	Marty Moore
Company Stage Manager	Lizzie Donaghy
Deputy Stage Manager	Vicky Eames
Assistant Stage Manager	Honor Ramsdale
Technical Assistant Stage Manager	Ben Coates
Stage Management Intern	Serena Ansong
Costume Supervisor	Isabelle Parzygnat
Props Supervisor	Mary Halliday
Wigs, Hair and Make-up Manager	Rosemary Williams
Wigs, Hair and Make-up Cover	Matilda Harbour
Lighting Operator	Susie Su
Lighting Programmer	Luca Panetta
Sound Operator	Michael Crowne
Video Programmer	Daberechi Ukoha-Kalu
Writer's Assistant	Frances Timberlake
Assistant Set Designer	Joy Chen
Assistant Lighting Designer	Amelia Fenwick
Assistant Sound Designer	Sarah Victoria
Production Photographer	Manuel Harlan
Story Consultant	Nick Yarris

Acknowledgements

This play would not exist without a debt of gratitude:

To Adrien Brody for reading the scripts I sent so quickly, for taking the risk on me. For saving me from myself in the rewriting process, for protecting my words and Nick's as if they were your own. Until they did become yours – from 'Yo' to 'run that chain' to the letter embedded in the center – to your delicate instinct given to the architecture of every line. Thank you for creating this alongside me in a way I've never gotten to work. The role of Nick now has the swagger of Queens, the tone of your humor, the balance of your taste.

To our original cast: Nana Mensah, your heart and attention to punctuation is unparalleled. To Michael Fox, Aidan Kelly, Posi Morakinyo, Cyril Nri, Ferdy Roberts, Tommy Sim'aan, for your moving commitment to an ensemble which elevated this show. And to all of the brilliant creative team for imprinting on the script in innumerable, indelible ways.

To Frances Timberlake, my assistant on so many projects, whose presence, organization, and opinions have changed my writing.

To Grace Duggan, for reading this play first and advocating for it and to Tim Sheader, for so boldly programming a world premiere in your first slot in your first season as artistic director. To Craig Gilbert for your advocacy and detailed thoughts.

To Nick Sidi, my British fairy godfather, whom I have my career and life in the UK to thank for, back from when you first read my play at the National ten years ago.

To my teacher and friend Sarah Ruhl, for all the check-ins as we both worked out our new shows and ourselves in London this fall.

To the late, great playwrights and my mentors, Tina Howe and Roy Kendall, for excavating my sense of story, which undoubtedly led me to this one.

To David Sington for sharing Nick Yarris's story with the world in your film; for saying yes to the email of this random playwright wanting to adapt it.

And mostly to Nicholas James Yarris, for letting me blend your words with mine; your life story with parts of myself. For our friendship and daily correspondence. When I once said: 'I'm sorry all of this happened to you', you responded with 'If you're still feeling sorry for me, you're missing the whole point.'

At the time of this writing, there are 2,213 people on Death Row in the United States today – each with their story.

Thank you to the audiences for listening to this one.

Lindsey Ferrentino

To get back up to the shining world from there
My guide and I went into that hidden tunnel;
And following its path, we took no care
o rest, but climbed: he first, then I so far
Through the round aperture I saw appear
Some of the beautiful things that Heaven bears
Where we came forth, and once more saw the stars.

Dante Alighieri, Inferno, XXXIV.134–140

Characters

NICK YARRIS [MAN 1]
JACKIE SCHAFFER
GUARD
VARIOUS INCARCERATED MEN ON DEATH ROW,
*who sing and play both the incarcerated and the innocent,
who double as the following characters:*
MAN 2: LIEUTENANT WALKER, SHERIFF 1, NICK'S
FATHER, POLICE OFFICER 2, CAPTAIN, BAILIFF,
ARTHUR CRAIG, JURY FOREMAN
MAN 3: JOE BULLEN, WAITER, PAWN-SHOP OWNER,
OFFICER BENJAMIN WRIGHT
MAN 4: WESLEY, SHERIFF 2, CLOAKROOM
ATTENDANT, EDDIE, PUBLIC DEFENDER
MAN 5: BUTCH, ANTHONY MANILLA, JIMMY
BRISBOIS, PROSECUTOR, CLERK, OLDER MAN
MAN 6: SOME GUARD, NICK'S MOTHER, POLICE
OFFICER 1, COP, JUDGE KELLY, JUDGE GILES

A forward slash (/) indicates overlapping dialogue.

Set

This world is fluid.

A playing space where scenes can assemble and collapse instantaneously, where the past can layer onto the present, where memories animate and disappear. A theater, but with barred windows, like a cell.

Where direct address is possible and the audience feels close.

Although the play is broken into 'scenes', that is just for rehearsal purposes. The production should have a feeling of continuous, flowing action.

This text went to press before the end of rehearsals and so may differ slightly from the play as performed.

1: LISTEN UP

MAN 1 *speaks to the audience – out of time*.

MAN 1. *Time...* can be a blisteringly fast thing, where in the blink of an eye – ten years are gone from your life, but the next week is agony.

It's like you look at your watch, and instead of a face – it's a calendar and it flips.
But then you look out the window... and it takes all day for the sun to go down...
I've always wanted to tell someone that.

A PRISON GUARD *speaks to the audience*.

GUARD. LISTEN UP!
I mean, you all should already know this, but I'll say it again.
No photography, no phone calls, no *pagers*.
For Chrissakes, just nothing that fucking *beeps*.
No matter how many times you've heard this, there *always* seems to be one.
And let's hope you went to the bathroom out in the lobby.
'Cause now that you're in here, that's fucking it. You gotta piss, cross your legs.
No cookies, no candies with crinkly-ass wrappers, no chicken chow mein.
Why would you *eat* in here? Eat at *home*.
No cigarettes, no crack cocaine, no needles, no drugs, no teddy bears.
If you want a female officer for the final pat-down, I don't have any free today, so try next week.

JACKIE. Excuse me?

GUARD. All visitors will dress *appropriately*.
Women, for the love of God, will wear a *bra*.

JACKIE (*to the audience*). Did – did he just check if I am?
– the *fuck*?

GUARD. But no bras with underwire, as you may not pass the final metal detector.
Nothing hoochie, nothing with writing – sexual, sarcastic, political, or otherwise.
Visitor last Monday took his sweater off to reveal a T-shirt that said:
'Surely not *everybody* was kung fu fighting.'
I'm not sure what that coded message means, but it wasn't funny, and humor has no place on a shirt.
(*To* JACKIE.) No pens, no paper.

JACKIE. – sorry, but we-we have special permission from the warden –

GUARD. You don't.

JACKIE. I – Sorry – I-I think we do.

The GUARD *takes* JACKIE*'s notebook, rips paper out, hands the paper back, keeps the metal binding.*

GUARD. No metal.
Okay! You will proceed into your assigned visiting booth, until your Death Row inmate is brought out. You will be informed when visiting time is up.

Lights shift. MEN *enter. The* GUARD *performs a security pat-down on* JACKIE.

Arms!

JACKIE (*to the audience*). The Pennsylvania prison system was developed by the *Quakers*.

GUARD. Spread 'em.

JACKIE (*to the audience*). Who – I don't know if you can tell, but the Quakers aren't a whole lotta fun.
A hundred and forty men in B-block. Level five, high maximum security. Each of them in solitary.

GUARD. One hour, then *time*!

Snippets from these one-on-one interviews, in and out of time, not realism. The MEN *speak to* JACKIE, *who sits at a table with a pen and paper.*

MAN 4. You! What's your name again?

JACKIE. You already asked me.

MAN 4. Sorry, I don't keep things in my head too / good.

JACKIE. Jackie –

MAN 5. I *like* that name.

JACKIE. Jackie Schaffer –

MAN 5. I'm gonna *roll* that name in my mouth.

MAN 6. My cell is thirty-eight square feet – bed, sink, no window, no natural / light.

MAN 1. I am in my cell twenty-three hours a day / except –

MAN 4. One hour outside, fucking / bullshit.

MAN 3. One hour a day to exercise by yourself.

GUARD. You're on Death Row. What do you need exercise for anyway?

MAN 2. And if the guards are being *pricks* /... or whatever –

GUARD. Hey!

MAN 2. If you have a problem with another guy, they put you both in a cage, knowing as soon as they walk off –

MAN 3 *takes a swing and a fight breaks out.*

MAN 6. – you'll beat the shit out of each other.

MAN 4. Guards do it to have some / fun.

MAN 1. Gladiator-ing, they call it.

MAN 2.... Yeah, I mean, I'd say it's not great.

JACKIE. – nice to meet you, too.

MAN 3. Can I borrow a piece of your paper?

GUARD. No touching the window.

MAN 3. I JUST WANNA GET RID OF MY GUM –

GUARD. Where the fuck did you get gum?

MAN 3. – oh shit.

JACKIE. Hiiii. My name is Jacqueline Schaffer?
I'm here with – with my friend Pamela Tucker? – the lead organizer of an abolitionist group from Pittsburgh?

MAN 4. Why you say everything like a question? Grow some balls.

JACKIE. We. Go around – monthly to visit *incarcerated people* such as / yourself –

MAN 1. You mean, prisoners on Death Row? It's okay – I know where I am.

JACKIE. – to, uh, check on their mental state? Since most people live on Death Row for over a decade –

MAN 2. *Decade?* Shit, I been here sixteen years.

MAN 5. Twelve.

MAN 6. Ever seen the line at the DMV?
That's to pay a parking ticket.
For the US to execute you, there's *a lot* more paperwork.

JACKIE. We're checking to see if the population of Death Row prisoners is treated fairly... Are you? Treated fairly?

MAN 1. What do *you* / think?

MAN 6. Fuck / no –

JACKIE. And you just tell me about yourself.

MAN 1. If you really want hear about it, you'll probably want to know what my lousy childhood was like, and how my parents were occupied and all before they had me, and all that David Copperfield kinda crap, but I don't feel like going into it, if you want to know the truth.

JACKIE. That is *not* your story.

MAN 1. Yes, it is.

JACKIE. That's *Catcher in the Rye*.

MAN 1. You've read that book...?

JACKIE. – yeah.

MAN 1. I've never known *anyone* who's read that book.

JACKIE. I've never known anyone who hasn't.

MAN 1. Have you spoken with anyone else here?

JACKIE. You are the sixth person I've interviewed at this facility today.

MAN 1. And –

JACKIE. And. The others are – lamenting how the coffee's mud. They don't usually open with Salinger.

MAN 1. Have you tasted the coffee?

JACKIE. What's your name?

MAN 1. Nick. You're new?

   MAN 1 *will be called* NICK *from here.*

JACKIE. No.

NICK. No?

JACKIE. Yes. No. Can you tell?

NICK. You're not wearing a wedding ring.

JACKIE. I'm not married.

NICK. Even the unmarried volunteers wear wedding rings. I think you get harassed less.

GUARD. VISITING TIME IS UP!

   JACKIE *moves her normal ring to her ring finger.*

   Alone, JACKIE *speaks to the audience.*

JACKIE. My friend *Pam* is the one who convinced me to start volunteering here...
She's that kind of friend *time* doesn't apply to – like she's

a lawyer, *and* a great mom, *and* runs literal marathons, *and* this entire prison volunteer program, *and* still, somehow, makes overnight oats.

I think of myself as a very high-functioning person, but I am not *Pam*.

GUARD. Arms!

JACKIE. ...Pam tells me it's better not to look up the crimes of the people I'm talking to.
You meet them today, not on the day that got them here.
If I'm supposed to treat them just like anybody else... Pam says it's better not to know.

GUARD. One hour, starting now.

MAN 2. You don't know anything about / me.

MAN 3. You can hook me up with some of them conjugals?

JACKIE. No. But Pam, for example, advocated for someone in Muncy. The prison had the wrong spelling of everyone on his visitation list. Eight years – no visitors, because of *typos*.

NICK. You're a lawyer?

JACKIE. PhD student.

NICK. In law?

JACKIE. Poetry.

NICK. You gotta be kidding me.

JACKIE. Is that a / problem?

NICK. I like Charles Bukowski as much as the next guy, but *poets* aren't who you want working your exoneration.

JACKIE. Are you hoping – to get exonerated?

NICK. I am not hoping for anything.

Beat.

JACKIE. So, tell me your story.

NICK. My story? It's long and loops around / and –

JACKIE. You could start from the beginning...

NICK. – it's hard.

JACKIE. Maybe because in life there isn't necessarily such a *thing* as a clear beginning?

NICK. There's always a beginning.

JACKIE. I just mean one thing leads to the next, and that leads to something else, and if you're not careful you – can wake up an entirely different person than you set out to be.

Beat.

NICK.... The day I arrived maybe?

JACKIE. I'll just / listen.

GUARD. Listen up for when I call *time*!

2: DAY ONE

NICK *speaks to* JACKIE. *As he tells his story, it plays out around him. He is both in the present, recalling the story, and in the past, reliving it.*

NICK (*to* JACKIE). I got into the prison, I don't know, about eleven a.m. –

MAN 5. Pulled up at night.

MAN 2. Noon.

MAN 4. Fall. I remember, 'cause I was like, 'I gotta get my winter clothes out from under my bed,' then I was like, 'oh yeah, no I don't.'

MAN 5. They line you up against this brick wall.

NICK. This guard, Lieutenant Walker walks right up to my face.

MAN 5. *Lieutenant Walker.*

MAN 4. *Lieutenant Walker.*

LIEUTENANT WALKER *turns to* NICK.

LIEUTENANT WALKER. There is no speaking in my prison, son.

NICK. I remember thinking – son? Why's this guard calling me, *son*.
Guys like him always want to call you, *son*.

LIEUTENANT WALKER. Dead men do not speak in my prison. You understand me, son?

NICK. Just like that. Nothing raised, nothing threatening.

LIEUTENANT WALKER. Dead men do not speak in my prison. You will soon be dead. Everyone you know and love is dead to you. In fact, you are dead now. You understand, or do we have a problem?

NICK (*to* LIEUTENANT WALKER). No, no / problem –

LIEUTENANT WALKER. I said dead men do not speak in my prison. Do you understand me?

NICK....

LIEUTENANT WALKER....

NICK....

LIEUTENANT WALKER....

NICK....

LIEUTENANT WALKER. Do you understand me?

NICK *nods*.

I said. DO. YOU. UNDERSTAND. ME.

NICK. – yes –

LIEUTENANT WALKER. What did I just say?!

LIEUTENANT WALKER *hits* NICK.

I guess you don't understand. But *you will*.

The prison door slams shut.

NICK. You are not allowed to communicate with *anyone*.
No one speaks.
You can hear the others cough, urinate, but no real *sound*.
You can still hear your mom crying at the trial.
Still smell the aftershave on the smug-ass prosecutor.
And every detail is eating you alive.
And if you talk to a neighbor, you're beaten by the guards.
And all the talking is in your head, and outside your head, the silence is – deadly.

The sound of prison silence.

And then my first time in the showers, I turned that corner, everyone's naked, and there's this guy with a sharpened pork chop bone, and he stabs this man in the liver.

MAN 4. The showers are the most *vulnerable* time. If you gonna get somebody, that's the place!

NICK. And this guy's bleeding, flopping, and they cut the water off, and all the guards beat all six of us senseless, drag us out.

JACKIE. *You saw that happen?*

NICK.... And then...

GUARD. LUNCH!

NICK. Then... they just serve *food*.
Like they serve lunch, like a routine day.

MAN 2. What you got, that nasty roast beef / today?

MAN 6. Food's so bad, they got you hoping to die. Just so you can get to that last / meal.

MAN 3. I heard John Wayne Gacy is asking for KFC. You can eat *anything* in the world and you ask for KFC? I think something must be wrong with that man.

MAN 4. Roast beef looks made of plastic.

MAN 6. Like it's still got the wrapper / on.

| MAN 5. Like why's it so fuckin' shiny – | MAN 4. Nasty. Nasty. Nasty. |

A MAN *steals a piece of bread from another* MAN*'s tray and a fight breaks out.*

GUARD. No speaking.

MAN 6. GET ME OUTTA HERE!!

Lights shift.

3: GET ME OUTTA HERE

JACKIE *packs up her notebook.*

NICK (*to* JACKIE). You don't believe me?

JACKIE. Sure, / I –

NICK. You *don't*, do you?

    NICK, *shortly after arriving in prison, speaks to his lawyer,* JOE BULLEN: *a middle-aged, militaristic man.*

JOE BULLEN. That's a great story, Nick.

NICK. Neither did my lawyer…

JOE BULLEN. Pork chop bone? Really?

NICK. Right from the start.

JOE BULLEN. Another great story.

NICK. It's not a story. It really happened.

JOE BULLEN. I hear you're always telling stories, son.

NICK. – what's with everyone calling me, *son*?
I saw a man *die* in the *showers*.

JOE BULLEN. You are a convicted murderer. What do you care?

NICK. You don't know *anything* about me.

JOE BULLEN. I know your whole story, 'cause I have read your file, beginning to end.
I'm Joe Bullen, your appellate attorney.

NICK. Oh – I – / sorry, listen – I –

JOE BULLEN. Sit. I have been appointed by Judge Giles to represent you on your direct appeal.

NICK *softens. Every thought pours out of his head.*

NICK. I been waiting seven months for this meeting. Where do / we start?

JOE BULLEN. Before you go on, know that I am a Christian... *and* an officer in the US Army, and so I fully support the death penalty.

NICK. You, *what*?

JOE BULLEN. You are guilty due to *overwhelming* evidence. You took the life from that woman, and so I believe – you too should die. It is my deepest held belief that society needs to prevent heinous crimes by not allowing killers and rapists to live. So unless you tell me anything outside of the public record, I am wasting my time here, Mr Yarris.

NICK (*to* JACKIE). Seven months in Huntingdon Prison. And *this* is who they sent me...?

JOE BULLEN. As a Christian man, I'll still file your appeal, but *know* where I stand.
There, but for the grace of God, go I.

NICK. A *Christian*, huh?

JOE BULLEN. Yes, sir. Sign / here –

NICK. Then, maybe you could help me with somethin' – as a Christian brother.

JOE BULLEN. Absolutely.

NICK.... Everyone in here is like, *attracted* to me, Joe. Like, should I go for it?

JOE BULLEN. That's not. Really my area. Of expertise.

JACKIE. You *said* that to him?

NICK. And there's this guard who pushed a note into my cell, wants to pay me to write him sex letters, twenty bucks a week. Like should I take the gig?

JOE BULLEN. Okay! I'm / not –

NICK. And when I went outside Monday mornin', they stick me in a cage next to Stevie Lloyd.
Know why that's a problem for me?

JOE BULLEN. Don't think I wanna know.

NICK. Stevie Lloyd's got three teeth. I tell Stevie how this guard sent me a letter with an offer for twenty bucks a week… Stevie stops me cold. Turns out… Stevie got the SAME letter… but *he* got offered *twenty-five* bucks for the same shit!! Five more than *my* offer, and the man's got no teeth!

NICK *bursts out laughing.*

JOE BULLEN. This is *funny* to you?

NICK. Know what the moral of that story is, Mr Bullen? Moral of the story is: I would rather have Stevie do my appeals, or that pervert guard, 'cause at least I *know* they're going to fuck me instead of the way you've just fucked me out of my appeal. Wanna pay me too, Mr Bullen? *You wanna pay me, too?!*

JOE BULLEN *quickly packs his paperwork.*

JOE BULLEN. I'm sure you're making your parents proud, Nick.

NICK. Wait! Wait –

JOE BULLEN *exits. The heavy metal door slams.* NICK *is stopped by this, silent.*

(*To* JACKIE.) I was only twenty-one. I shouldn't have –
(*Calling off to* JOE BULLEN.) *Wait!*
(*To* JACKIE.) Wait, you're leaving?

JACKIE. It's late.
   It's far for me, the drive.

NICK. Oh. Okay.

4: VISIT 2

Alone, JACKIE *speaks to the audience.*

JACKIE. Everyone in here has their *story*.
   It's really hard to know what's true. Their stories can be so specific, I can almost see them. But specificity can be a trick of the deceptive…
   Because you think, 'no good liar can lie that well' – but that's exactly what good liars do.

GUARD. One hour.

JACKIE. The truth is… it's hard to know.

GUARD. Starting now.

NICK. After that first meeting with my lawyer, I lived in silence for more than two years.
   Seven hundred and forty-eight days,
   I didn't say one *single* word.
   Until drugs were discovered in the choir room… That's when *everything changed*.

5: I WISH IT WOULD RAIN

Lights shift. A big one this time. Maybe music.
NICK *stands and sets the scene, in and out of the present/past.*

NICK. Okay, so –

In another part of the prison, there were some guys locked up for more minor things.

They still had life, but they were allowed to take classes, or sing in a prison choir.

But when the guards discovered drugs in the music room, they moved these guys into empty cells on Death Row while they were being questioned.

Since none of them were gonna rat, the guards were gonna ship them off to different prisons, break up the choir, break up the band – some Yoko-Ono-ish-type punishment.

To the other members of the choir, it really didn't matter.

But there were these two men with a bond that was *special*.

Lights to WESLEY *and* BUTCH. WESLEY *hums under the following.*

Wesley and *Butch*.

Wesley met Butch when they were children in West Philly, where Butch was a foster child. Wesley was gay. Butch said he wasn't gay, he just loved Wesley.

Butch began doing some pretty serious crime, and got thrown into prison for life...

Wesley went *nuts* without him.

Butch was the only thing in his life that protected him from all the people who knew he was *weak* without Butch.

So, Wesley began committing *deliberate* crimes... just so he could get locked up with Butch. It's still... the most romantic thing I've ever heard. And it worked!

They got themselves put into the same cell. And in prison, where homosexuality is *accepted*, no one bothered them. So, they built this – sort of beautiful life together, here...

The MEN *hum.*

That is – until drugs were discovered in the music room.

SOME GUARD. Hey, you're going!

NICK. The guard on duty at nine o'clock started tormenting Wesley.

SOME GUARD. We're splitting you two up! You're going to opposite ends of Pennsylvania. You will *never* see each other again.

NICK. Wesley couldn't even say goodbye to Butch – the love of his life – 'cause they'd been separated into two cells, and 'cause of the 'no talking' rule.

In the cell, WESLEY *goes crazy, punching the wall.*

But *just* before they were about to be shipped out, this… *voice* took over.…

The voice of WESLEY, *virtuosic and pure, rises above the torturous silence; something like David Ruffin's 'I Wish it Would Rain'.*

The MEN *crane their necks to listen.*

We *knew* the penalty. For making *any* sound. Let alone *singing*.

Keys jingling. Hurried footsteps as SOME GUARD *intervenes. The singing gets louder, the* MEN *are rioting.*

SOME GUARD. What are you doing singing in my block? I will beat your head in.
If you don't stop that singing right now I will beat your head in!! Are you listening to me? Stop! Singing! Calling backup! Code ten–thirty-four!

LIEUTENANT WALKER *comes running.*

LIEUTENANT WALKER. HOLD IT!

Everyone stops singing.

NICK. Lieutenant Walker comes running down.

LIEUTENANT WALKER. Hold it right now!!

LIEUTENANT WALKER *looks around.*

I'm off in twenty minutes. If there is a noise on this block from *anyone* after I leave, my guards will beat every man's head in.
You are on Death Row and no one will care if you die.
But for now... you got twenty minutes.
Finish that song, inmate.

Beat. SOME GUARD *turns, like* LIEUTENANT WALKER *has lost his mind.*

SOME GUARD. What the / f– ?!

LIEUTENANT WALKER. Twenty minutes isn't long, son, so you better *sing*.

LIEUTENANT WALKER *and* SOME GUARD *exit. The gates shut behind them. Other* MEN *join the singing, percussive drumming on the bars, harmonizing.*

NICK. And Wesley came right back in, like he'd never stopped –

The PRISON CHOIR *are now singing with* WESLEY.

And then, out of nowhere –

A high falsetto voice, singing The Temptations's 'Just My Imagination (Running Away with Me)'.

BUTCH *is singing.*

Wait, is that – *Butch*?

Butch's six-foot-four, two hundred and forty pounds – big, jagged scar down the side of his face. I am *terrified* of this man –

– but to hear him *sing* in that beautiful voice... as his way of showing love for someone being taken from him –

– made me want someone to care for *me* in that way. The way that *singing* was worth it, even when singing can get your head beat in.

The song continues as SOME GUARD *handcuffs* WESLEY, *removing him from the block. One* MAN *continues singing.*

They shipped Wesley and Butch off later that night.
The next day, a few guys in the cells were talking, and when the guard went by? This time...?

SOME GUARD. You can talk, just not too loud, alright?

NICK. They weren't going to torture us with silence anymore.
So... that was somethin.'

JACKIE looks at NICK.

JACKIE. That is a – beautiful story, Nick.
But it's still not yours...
Sorry, I didn't realize what time it was. I have to –
I don't know if I can come next week –

Lights shift. Another day.

NICK (*to the audience*). But she did.

As song concludes, JACKIE *turns to the other* MEN.

6: 'WHAT CAN YOU TELL ME?'

JACKIE (*to* MAN 2). What can you tell me about Nick Yarris?

MAN 3. What, like if we're friends? This ain't *The Shawshank Redemption*, bitch, we're in solitary.

MAN 4. Nick goes by / Harry.

MAN 6. Harry / Houdini!!

MAN 5. Oh, everybody knows Harry / Houdini...

MAN 3. The legend / of –

MAN 4. Nick. Is / *crazy.*

MAN 2. *Everybody* knows that / story.

JACKIE.... Why do they call him / that?

MAN 2. 'Cause of that day of his appeal / trial.

MAN 3. Nick's lawyer was trying to get his death sentence reduced to life.

NICK. Hold on, hold on. *Two years* I waited for my appeals trial. But then these sheriffs finally came.

Two SHERIFFS *enter.*

7: RUN

The SHERIFFS *start cuffing* NICK *for transport.*

SHERIFF 1. Jerry Berndt is a g'damn / hero.

SHERIFF 2. – finally stopped playing like they were *asleep* –

SHERIFF 1. – 'bout time Penn State got some respect. Jerry Berndt is a g'damn hero –

SHERIFF 2. Hands.

SHERIFF 1. Let's go.

NICK. They get me into the car.
One sheriff driving up front. I'm in the back with the other.

SHERIFF 1. We will share no more in '84.

SHERIFF 2. We will tell no lies in '85.

NICK (*to* JACKIE). Like, I don't really care about sports, but I was *desperate* to speak to someone.
(*To the* SHERIFFS.) So, Penn State's doing well this year?

SHERIFF 2. *Are* they doing / *well*.

SHERIFF 1. Are they doing / well.

SHERIFF 2. I cried.

SHERIFF 1. You cried? I / cried.

SHERIFF 2. I cried myself to / sleep!

SHERIFF 1. I could *kiss* head coach, Jerry Berndt.

NICK. Six hours later, these guys are somehow *still* talkin' football!

SHERIFF 1. – whole season was a piece of *art*!

NICK (*to himself*). – Jesus Christ –

SHERIFF 1. Hey, I gotta take a leak.

NICK. We pull into a gas station to find a bathroom. It's nearly pitch dark.

Suddenly, NICK *is outside in the snow.*

SHERIFF 1. *Damn* it's cold –

SHERIFF 2. Jerry Berndt wouldn't care about the cold, now would / he?

SHERIFF 1. Not while kissin' on his championship ring!

NICK. The driver stays in the car. The other sheriff goes in with me. I'm pissing, *all* I'm thinking about is getting back in that warm-ass car.

SHERIFF 1 *and* NICK *pee against the back wall of the theater.*

So, I head right back. But the sheriff behind the wheel doesn't see the other cop. Doesn't know if I killed his partner or what. All he's thinking is a Death Row convicted murderer is running at him, unescorted.

SHERIFF 2. Hold it right there! HOLD IT, HOLD / IT!!

NICK. Everything stops.
He pulls his weapon, I panic – and, I don't know if you've ever had a gun pulled on you, but… you run!
He fires!

Gunshot.

SHERIFF 2. Shots fired!

NICK. I go down. I hit the ground.

SHERIFF 2. Shots fired!

NICK. I'm not shot?! What the fuck, he missed?! You missed!? And it starts like this attitude in me, this unlocked joy.

The MEN *and* SHERIFFS *search for* NICK *with flashlights.*

SHERIFF 2. He's / up!

SHERIFF 1. He's / running!

SHERIFF 2. He's running to the diner next door!

NICK. I figured if I was running directly at the window full of pedestrians, he can't shoot.

SHERIFF 1 *and* SHERIFF 2. He's running!

NICK. Cops are yelling at each other –

SHERIFF 2. What about *you*?!

SHERIFF 1. What *about* me?!   SHERIFF 2. Talkin' about Jerry g'damn Berndt the whole time!!

JACKIE. Nick, is all this *true*?? Why would you *run* on the way to your own appeal?
Wait, wait. What about your handcuffs –

NICK (*to* JACKIE). Took 'em off.

JACKIE (*in disbelief*). Oh, come on. How'd you take off your handcuffs?

Magically, NICK*'s handcuffs drop to the ground.*

NICK. Like this.

SHERIFF 1. We need backup checking the entirety of Beaver Falls.

SHERIFF 2. We have an escaped Death Row prisoner alert.

Police sirens and lights overwhelm NICK.

NICK. I see the building to my right has some sort of flag.
A police station. You'd have to be crazy to hide at the actual police station. But… get this… that's what I do.
I huddle down in the snow behind the station… and I wait.
And they never look for me there.
Fuckin' idiots.

NICK *moves through the snow in the dark, quiet.*

Damn, it's cold.
– going into these bends.
I'm gonna freeze, I gotta get up.
I come flying out of that parking lot and –

SHERIFF 2. I said backup now! *Now!*

NICK. Fuck, no, no, no I think they saw me.
Three hours of this.
My feet split open.
My calves erupt.
My hamstrings pull.
I follow railroad tracks, walking on broken feet for five miles.

Snow continues to fall around him.

8: THE ESCAPE, BUT STILL NOT FREE

NICK. I steal a car. A 1965 green Mustang, *beautiful*.
If you ever find yourself an escaped Death Row prisoner…
just go for the Mustang.
I call my mom from a phone booth. I still call my mom as much as I can.

JACKIE. Me too.

NICK. *Moms*, huh?

From nowhere, NICK'S MOTHER *appears.*

NICK'S MOTHER. Nicky, is that you?

NICK. Please, Mom, you gotta help / me.

NICK'S MOTHER. Take these clothes, baby – two hundred bucks, and this Philly Eagles ski cap.

NICK. Mom. I'm trying to go incognito. Can't you gimme *any* piece of clothing that isn't a dead giveaway as to where I'm from?

NICK'S MOTHER. Baby, no. It's the *Eagles*.
   They're good luck.

NICK. I drive to New York City.
   I get a hotel room in a flophouse on the Bowery.
   And it has a *bathtub*.
   I have institutional prison sock threaded into the torn tissue of my feet.
   I – can't even venture out for three days, I literally can't walk.
   I soak.
   How did this happen?

JACKIE. I start reading what I can find on his escape. Which isn't much. It's twenty years ago at this point – DAY FOUR. THE SEARCH CONTINUES FOR DEATH ROW ESCAPEE.
   I drive to my school's library, looking at old newspapers, night after night, when I'm supposed to be writing my thesis. Day FIFTEEN. PENNSYLVANIA DEATH ROW ESCAPEE NICK YARRIS STILL ON THE LOOSE.

Eventually, NICK *gets out of the tub, limps out into the New York street.*

NICK. I go out.
   I can still hardly walk, so I boost a bicycle and *ride* uptown.
   I haven't been on a bike since I was a kid…
   – felt *so good* to do something *normal*.
   Totally free.
   Until I pass Macy's and see all these TVs.

NICK *watches footage of himself on the news.*

TV ANNOUNCER 1 (*voice-over*). After a helicopter chase that went over several hours, escaped killer, Nicholas Yarris, is still at large.

NICK. And I realize.
   – oh –
   I am *not* free.

TV ANNOUNCER 2 (*voice-over*). A nationwide manhunt is currently underway as the police continue their search for Yarris.

NICK. I am on the FBI's Most-Wanted List.

TV ANNOUNCER 3 (*voice-over*). Police have said Yarris poses a threat to the public, and urge people to call 911.

NICK. I am temporarily out on a leash, and if they catch me I'll catch a bullet, too.

JACKIE (*to the audience*). *Pam* keeps calling me. She noticed I only seem to visit one person now.
She asks what the issue is I'm taking up on his behalf.
I tell her, 'I don't have one yet.'
'I'm not getting *attached*, but I'm getting *involved*. Isn't that what you trained me to do?' *Pam*.

Back with NICK *and* JACKIE.

NICK. Are you still with me?

JACKIE. Yeah.

NICK. You went somewhere in your head. Where did you go?

JACKIE. I'm here.
I'm listening.

NICK. While I'm on the run, I go to this real upscale restaurant.

WAITER. Welcome to the Cheesecake Factory.

NICK. No – upscale, like *fancy* –

Tinkly music, as NICK *steps inside a fancy restaurant.*

WAITER. Good evening, sir. Table for one?

NICK (*to* WAITER *in a 'fancy' voice*). *Don't mind if I do.*

(*To* JACKIE.) I see this rich guy go to the bathroom without his jacket, so I walk to his table, and – I steal his jacket.
He's got a wallet in his pocket.
So I go to the cloakroom.

CLOAKROOM ATTENDANT. Good evening, sir. Do you have your ticket?

NICK. Uh, yes, I do! That mink there, that is my wife's jacket. To the left, the fur.

CLOAKROOM ATTENDANT. Oh, absolutely, sir.

NICK is handed a mink coat and puts a tip in the jar.

NICK. *Don't mind if I do.*
(*To* JACKIE.) I tip the coatcheck.

JACKIE (*laughing*). You *tipped*?

NICK. Yes? I am not an animal.
I use the guy's credit card to buy a last-minute plane ticket, and land in a place of freedom, of magic, the happiest place on earth...
Orlando, Florida.
I think: Never again in handcuffs.
I think: I'll buy a raft, a cooler of beer, some Doritos, float out into the ocean wearing that mink coat, and have one last blow-out party beneath that big, hot sky. Then cut my wrists and wait for the sharks to come.

JACKIE. You are *very* dramatic.

NICK. But then I remembered my little mom looking at me going...

NICK'S MOTHER. *Live,* son, *live*.

NICK. So, I had to. Keep running. But I needed *money*. So, I hailed a –

(*Hailing a cab*.) – Taxi! Pawn shop.

9: FLORIDA, MAN

The ding of the pawn-shop bell.

PAWN-SHOP OWNER. How y'all doin'?

NICK. The pawn-shop owner was obviously a criminal.
Like, I'm not a great people reader, but it didn't take an Einstein.

PAWN-SHOP OWNER. Welcome to *Pawn Plaza*. Ya'll findin' everything okay?

NICK. He had the two identifying traits of a criminal: shifty eyes... and a mullet.

PAWN-SHOP OWNER. I got ten brand-new VCRs for sale I found on the side of the road!

NICK. I wanna sell you this mink coat.

PAWN-SHOP OWNER. You got a driver's license?

NICK. You got a license to be sellin' *ten* brand-new VCRs?

PAWN-SHOP OWNER. Without ID, alls I can give ya is a hundred bucks.

NICK. For mink.

PAWN-SHOP OWNER. It's Florida, man. How many people lookin' for fur?

NICK. It's worth five grand!

PAWN-SHOP OWNER. I'll give you four *grand*, if you give me a receipt for its original purchase... and your ID?

NICK. Fine. I'll take the hundred bucks. But you gotta throw in a gun.

PAWN-SHOP OWNER. *Gun??*
– oh, yeah, fine, sure I can throw in couple guns. Florida, man. No problem-o.

They shake hands. NICK *hands over the fur coat, collects his money and a small gun.*

JACKIE. What did you need a gun for, Nick?

PAWN-SHOP OWNER. No bullets, though. Unless you do a little thing for me...

NICK. I'll get bullets somewhere else –

PAWN-SHOP OWNER. You won't.
'Cause after you leave, I'll report the gun stolen, 'cause you ain't got a receipt for that either. Unless, you do me this favor.

NICK. I don't want to get involved.

PAWN-SHOP OWNER. Man buys bullets *to* get involved.
You'll go pay a visit to this guy I know, named Anthony Manilla.
Nothing illegal, nothin' creepy. He's just got a collection of gold coins I want –

NICK. Coins? What're you, a fucking pirate?

PAWN-SHOP OWNER. Worth three hundred and fifty dollars each.

NICK. And he'll just give 'em to me?

PAWN-SHOP OWNER. He'll give 'em to ya, if I give you the bullets.

Beat. NICK *takes the bullets, while looking at* JACKIE.

NICK (*to* JACKIE). I'm a good guy, okay?

JACKIE (*to the audience*). Usually with men it's only the bad ones that go out of their way to tell you they're good.

NICK (*to* JACKIE). Actually I am. I really am.
I just do stupid, stupid things.

NICK *shouts to* ANTHONY MANILLA.

Yo, Anthony! Anthony Manilla! Hey! That / you?

ANTHONY MANILLA. I know you?

NICK. Remember me? High school? We were on the same team!

ANTHONY MANILLA. Wrestling?

NICK. You were *good*, man.

ANTHONY MANILLA. Aww, yeah, thank you.

NICK (*to* JACKIE). I'm lying... And poor Anthony Manilla pretended he recognized me in that fake-ass way people do when they don't?

ANTHONY MANILLA. YOU LOOK GREAT! Whatcha up / to?

NICK (*to* ANTHONY). Oh MAN, you look great, too.
(*To* JACKIE.) I mean. He didn't. He looked like a crackhead, so I made up this story.
(*To* ANTHONY.) I got a bunch of pills, bro. Wanna go do 'em at your place?

ANTHONY MANILLA. Pills? Fuck, yeah!

NICK. Get in my car, I'll drive you home.
(*To* JACKIE.) I am *good* at telling stories.

NICK *pulls the gun out on* ANTHONY.

Okay, freeze! You're gonna give me your money, you're gonna give me your Rolex, all that diamond jewelry – take it off, you're gonna run that chain. That's good. And what we're gonna do is go in your house, and you're gonna give me all your gold coins.

ANTHONY MANILLA. Not my coins, man! ANYTHING BUT MY COINS!

NICK (*to* JACKIE). I tie him up with some old T-shirts, throw him in my trunk. But what I don't realize is the latch don't close.
Three red lights later... Anthony jumps out. Lookin' like the *mummy* who's unravelled, running through traffic, knocking on windows. Shit was INSANE.

ANTHONY MANILLA. He's robbing me! He wants my coins!! ANYTHING BUT MY COINS!

NICK. These tourists are staring at the mummy yelling about coins, so I just *gun* it past the red light, fly right up I-4.
Two-thirty in the morning I get to Daytona Beach.
I've been an escaped con for twenty-five days.
I can't get a hotel room anywhere, my eyes are all gravelly, I'm *exhausted*, so I put the seat back, and –

10: THE ARREST

NICK *wakes to two* POLICE OFFICERS.

POLICE OFFICER 1. Hey, buddy.

POLICE OFFICER 2. Come on, son.

NICK. No, no, no, no, no.
Cop's motioning like this.

> POLICE OFFICER 1 *gestures that* NICK *should roll down his window.*

(*To* JACKIE.) Like what a stupid motion that is. Like what is that.
So, I roll down the window...

POLICE OFFICER 1. You hear anybody screaming?

NICK. Screaming? What?

POLICE OFFICER 1. Some domestic dispute. Bikers.

> NICK *is suddenly terrified, which makes him manic.*

NICK. No, yeah! Bikers! Fuck! The worst! Fuck *bikers*, huh?!

POLICE OFFICER 2.... Is there a problem here, son?

NICK. Nah, nah, nah, no – I just hope she's okay! Worried –

POLICE OFFICER 1. Why you seem so nervous, huh?

NICK. – Is this illegal? I didn't know if I could just park and / sleep –

POLICE OFFICER 2. Hey, Burke, there's a gun in the backseat.

> POLICE OFFICER 1 *pulls out his gun.*

NICK. Fuck...

POLICE OFFICER 1. Outta the / car!

POLICE OFFICER 2. Name –

NICK. Bob – *Coins*.

POLICE OFFICER 1. Your last name is *Coins*.

NICK. Oh... O'Coin. O'Coin.
  I'm – Irish.

POLICE OFFICER 2. Top of the mornin' to ya.

POLICE OFFICER 1. Book him.

11: BOOK HIM

A metal door slams.

NICK. So. I'm sitting in a Daytona Jail as Bob O'Coin, waiting to see if they figure out who I am, and I'm – just *spent*.

COP. One call. Make it quick. Two minutes.

  NICK *picks up a phone*. NICK'S FATHER *answers*.

NICK. Dad??

NICK'S FATHER. Nick??

NICK. Hi, Dad, sorry / I –

NICK'S FATHER. Where are you? They been looking for you for a *month*. We're worried / sick.

NICK'S MOTHER. That Nicky?

NICK. Mom – !!

NICK'S MOTHER. Nicky, hiii – I love you. We should never have kicked / you out.

NICK'S FATHER. You used to be so / *good* –

NICK'S MOTHER. Remember – you loved board games, riding your bike –

NICK'S FATHER. – and were so shy with / girls.

NICK. I love you. I love you both.

NICK'S FATHER. We're proud of you, son.

NICK (*to* JACKIE). *Son*. In the way it's meant to be said. (*Into the phone.*) *You're proud?*

NICK'S MOTHER. *Always*. Nicky, give 'em hell!

NICK. Listen, Pop, call the FBI. Tell 'em where I'm at, okay? The jig's up. I wanna turn myself in.
(*Back to* JACKIE.) Once cops found out who I was, they were arranging for my transfer back to PA, they stuck me on Death Row in Florida. And guess who was in there?

JACKIE. Who?

NICK. Ted mother-fucking Bundy.

JACKIE. *Come on*.

NICK. I'm tellin' you, every mass murderer on Death Row was *terrified* of Bundy. I was eager to get back to Pennsylvania. And you *know* it's bad in Florida if I'd rather be with the Quakers.

JACKIE. – The more ludicrous your stories are, the more I find out they're true.

NICK. You been looking me up?

JACKIE. Oh, just your escape.

NICK. You – didn't read anything else about / me?

GUARD. Time's / up –

NICK. You said I had two / minutes –

GUARD. That *was* two / minutes –

NICK. No, it fucking wasn't!!

| GUARD. What did you say to me – ?? | NICK (*to* JACKIE). What else did you read about me? |

NICK *starts being dragged off.*

JACKIE. Nothing, / nothing –

GUARD. Time's up, / Yarris!

NICK. That was not even a fucking / minute!!

JACKIE. Nick – !

NICK. I get one hour, once a week. This is it, give me my MINUTE, PLEASE –

The GUARD *drags* NICK *off, beating him violently.*

Long beat.

Alone, JACKIE *turns to the audience.*

JACKIE. I feel myself splitting. Down the middle.
There's the part of me that's – worried about him.
And the part that's worried about what the fuck I am doing.
I have read his whole story... about what he's done.
...And I saw pictures of the body, too –
...
But like anything you do that's – *questionable*, it doesn't stop you from doing it.
You just do it with the awareness of how questionable it is.
Like I'm watching myself very carefully now.
Getting in my car.
Driving straight back to the prison.

12: INTO THE TUNNEL

Another day, JACKIE *sees* NICK, *bloodied*.

NICK. Why are you here? What do you / want?

JACKIE. – your face – Nick, your / *face* –

NICK. I get *no* visitors. And yet you keep coming / back.

JACKIE. – what happened to / you?

NICK. I know *nothing* about you, except you're a writer, right?

JACKIE. Your *nose* looks / broken –

NICK. You sure you're not just looking for a good story?

JACKIE. No.

NICK. Am I *research* to you?

JACKIE. *No, no.*

NICK. Then, I'd rather hear about you a little.

JACKIE. Oh. I – I don't. / Usually –

NICK. I mean you don't have to. If you're not allowed –

JACKIE. It's not that I'm not / *allowed* –

NICK. I'm just alone all day.
 Every day, the only voice I hear is my own, narrating everything I do.
 So, any – anything you wanna share would be –
 music.

13: MUSIC

The MEN *hum beneath a mash-up of* JACKIE *and* NICK*'s various conversations. Many days. Not realism.*

JACKIE. I am Jackie Schaffer.
 I am thirty-three years old.
 I'm older than the rest of my class, 'cause I travelled for some years playing violin.

NICK. *Violin??*

JACKIE. It's two hundred and seventy-five miles from Pittsburgh to here.
 It's a beautiful drive.
 There are these *mountains* –
 Laughlintown. Which I always read on the map as Laughintown. Which I like.

 After the tunnel, I listen to music. Really loudly. Seal. Don't judge me.

I drive into the foothills of Chestnut Ridge.
There's this little museum there for the Underground Railroad. This tiny, old church with a sign that says how Pennsylvania was the first free state north of the Mason–Dixon Line, and how *hundreds* of slaves would cross to their new lives, and the *first* thing they'd see... is that small church I look at now, eating my McDonald's in the parking lot.
I sit there and think about whatever freedom is...

GUARD. Time.

NICK. Come on.

JACKIE. I'll come back.

NICK (*to the audience*). In this four-by-five-foot visiting booth, she walks in and we *talk*.

JACKIE. I have just one younger brother. Lives in Austin.

NICK (*to the audience*). Week after week. Through the metal mesh in the glass wall between us.

JACKIE. I'm close with my mom, not my dad.

NICK (*to the audience*). *My* chair is bolted to the ground, hers is free.

JACKIE. I had to cut him out based on who he voted for. Which seems like an overreaction, but who even am I if the things I say matter to me – don't?

NICK (*to the audience*). She has this way of fidgeting with her pencil that I look forward to. I guess she's nervous.

JACKIE. I'm not nervous.

NICK. Then why do you always sit up so straight?

JACKIE. That's – my posture. From violin. Why does the way I sit always seem to annoy people?

NICK. She's nervous.

Another day.

GUARD. One hour. Then time.

JACKIE. Hi.

NICK. Hi.

Another day.

JACKIE. Chamber music, mostly.

NICK *laughs*.

NICK. People actually *paid* you for that?

JACKIE *(laughing)*. Wow, Jesus. You must really hate violin.

NICK. Nah, I just – I've never known anyone who – *a poet and a musician*.

JACKIE. I'm... somewhat good at a lot of things, and – I think I might not be great at anything.

Beat.

NICK. I got no respectable talents.

Beat. Another day.

I looked it up – it's called a dilettante.

JACKIE. I am *not* a dilettante.
Have you read every book here?

NICK. The first thousand took me three years.

JACKIE. You've read a *thousand* books?

NICK. I'm so glad I'd been a drug addict, 'cause I got *addicted* to books.

If I don't know a word, I just look it up, and keep repeating it in different sentences. I have forty-word days, fifty-word days.

Like, '*incredulous*.' That's a good word for me. The state of being unwilling to believe something.

JACKIE. Are you? Incredulous?

NICK. I just intend to speak eloquently when they give me my last words. I don't want to die in ignorance.

JACKIE. Oh!   GUARD. TIME!

> JACKIE *starts to leave, then turns back to* NICK.

JACKIE. I – could bring you some books? That they don't have here.

NICK. I'd like that.

More days.

Yo, fuck Nabokov. That guy is a complete perv –

JACKIE. Well, *Lolita* hasn't exactly aged well.

NICK. I have to say that is a *weird* first choice for our prison book club, Jackie. Jesus Christ.

JACKIE. Sorry.

Another day.

I can't believe you finished! I'm still on chapter fifteen!

NICK. I wished it was longer.

JACKIE. It's *War and Peace*. No one has said that, ever.

Another book, another day.

I haven't read it since eighth grade, I had braces.

NICK. Made me miss having a dog.

JACKIE. I wish I could bring mine to visit you. Dottie.

NICK. *Dottie, the dog!!*

JACKIE. – had her for ten years. Through two relationships, an engagement, grad school. She's the story of my decade.

NICK. Mine was Jocko. Beautiful sheep dog, but he ran away.
So strange to think I'll never have another dog again...
Or a kid. Or get married. Or fall in love...

JACKIE. Think you've got the order wrong.

NICK. – You were engaged?

JACKIE. Oh. Um. Yeah. Until last year.
It felt like I spent all my days with just one person.
And sometimes one person can feel like a whole world...
And sometimes one person can feel like – like – just one person.

NICK. Right. Which is this?

Long beat.

Sorry.

JACKIE. Sorry – I don't actually know why I...
I can't come for a couple weeks. I've got papers due –

NICK. Oh. I'm sorry if / – was too personal. I do that.

JACKIE. No, you didn't, you didn't – Sorry.
You – you could call? Me. At home?

Long beat.

NICK. – Really?

JACKIE. Probably easier.

NICK. ... It's collect, though.

JACKIE. It would just save me the drive. And it's cheaper than gas.

NICK. Sure.

JACKIE (*to the audience*). I give him my number. I immediately regret it, because now he can look up where I live.

PRE-RECORDED MESSAGE. Do you accept a collect call from the Department of Corrections, state of Pennsylvania?

JACKIE. Yes.

Sound in the background of Jackie's apartment.

NICK. Oh, sorry, do you have someone over?

JACKIE. No, it's um – TV. It's – the show is called, *Cheers*.

NICK. *Cheers*? That's what you're watching?

JACKIE. It's on in the background. I'm not really watching –

NICK. Well, what's it about?

JACKIE. These friends who – sort of just – hang out in a bar.

NICK. Yeah? Are we – friends?

PRE-RECORDED MESSAGE. Do you accept a collect / call –

Another day, another call.

JACKIE. It's called *Seinfeld*?

NICK. *Seinfeld*? What's it about?

JACKIE. More friends – who sort of just – hang out in an apartment.

NICK. Man, what the hell has happened to TV?!

They laugh.

JACKIE.... Yeah... we're friends, Nick...
We're friends.

Another day.

(*To the audience*.) I start to *prefer* talking to him on the phone.
The prison – sort of – falls away.
And I'm just talking to a *person*, sitting on my couch.

Another day.

I-I think you might have been right, by the way.
I may have come here, at first, hoping for a story.
I think I'm always on the hunt for something *authentic* to write about?
But what does that even mean?
No one would want my story about some white guy I met in prison.
You are the *last* person I thought I'd end up still talking to...

NICK. I can't tell if that's an insult or a compliment.

JACKIE. That's not why I'm here. *Anymore*, anyway.

NICK. Good.

JACKIE. Good.

NICK. Good.

Another day.

You messed this up for me, you know. I had an okay thing going for myself in here, reading and filling my time. Now I just wonder when I might get to see you again...

JACKIE (*to* NICK). Yeah, we're – we're friends, Nick. I promise... We're *friends*.

NICK (*to the* GUARD). We're friends.

GUARD. TIME.

Sudden shift into another day.

14: WHY DID YOU MAIL ME THIS?

JACKIE. – Why did you mail me this?

JACKIE *and* NICK, *across from each other.* JACKIE *holds a newspaper article. Realism.*

NICK. Did you read it? I ripped it out, sent it straight to you.

JACKIE. Why did you send me this article, Nick?

NICK. 'Newly developed DNA science makes a big splash in the crime *world*.' If DNA is getting people convicted, why can't it get people released?

JACKIE. I'm sure DNA *could*, if your DNA isn't on the crime scene.
I've been coming here for *eight months* now, and you have / never –

NICK. I didn't kill that woman.

JACKIE. – *What?*

NICK. I got two things to tell you.
One: I did not kill Mrs Craig. I had *nothing* to do with it. I am completely innocent of every single charge.

And two:
I'm falling in love with you…

Beat.
Beat.

JACKIE. Okay, let's –
Let's handle the first one first.

NICK. I am in love with you. I love the way you pick your nail polish while we talk, and leave behind these little bright colors, and the way you think, and your crazy posture, your terrible taste in television, and your – all of it. Just – you. I've never been in love before, but I know what this is. And – it was never gonna be worth saying out loud. But now – but *now*…

JACKIE. Nick. We – need to prove your innocence.
If we can do that –

NICK. You said *we*.

JACKIE. If *we* can prove you are innocent…
Then.
Then.
Then we can worry about the second half of what you just said.

Beat.

GUARD. Time.

Quick blackout.

15: NOT ME

A song from all of the MEN. *Loud, arresting, vibrant. The music should feel so huge, it takes your breath away. Maybe Led Zeppelin's 'Ten Years Gone', or a more in-your-face arrangement of Bruce Cockburn's 'Pacing the Cage'. Or something better.*

From this cacophony, JACKIE *talks to the audience.*

JACKIE (*to the audience*). I am *not that* person, okay?
Prison-Pen-Pals, Convict-Mailbag – these are *real* things.
That's *not* what this story is. That is *not* the story I would ever tell myself about myself.
I don't tell my mom, or my friends, because I am well aware of what this sounds like.
He said he's falling in love with me…
The word *falling* always feels strange.
It feels more like – *noticing*?
Notice how they feel known to you, even though they're not.
Notice how he listens.
And how he notices everything about me.
Notice I picture scenes with Nick, outside of his cell.
We're at Bed Bath and Beyond on a Sunday morning, but I forget the twenty-percent-off coupon at home, but because it's Bed Bath and Beyond… they just give you *another*… for free! I love that place.

We go to Bed Bath and Beyond, because I can picture a home. With sheets and towels.
I don't know why, but I picture our *toothbrushes* touching.
They stand next to each other every night. While we sleep next to each other in a big bed.
And we'll get a *dog*.
Like Jocko, that dog that ran away when he was a kid.
I am *attached* to these memories that have not even happened yet…

I see our lives unfolding and
folding laundry and
holding hands

and Bed. And Bath.
And Beyond.
And Beyond.
And *Beyond*.

A loud buzzing.

GUARD. Time's up.

NICK. *No.* JACKIE. No.

GUARD. Time's / up.

JACKIE. No, / *please* –

GUARD. NO TOUCHING THE WINDOW!

NICK. Goddamnit. Next / week.

JACKIE. *Call.*

NICK. Next week. Come.
  Please.

JACKIE (*to the audience*). I go to get in my car. It's so quiet. And I'm standing there with the door still open, unable to leave.
Until I'm driving home alone through the endless tunnel.

Again.

To my house that felt like a home *before*, but now all I notice is there's *one* toothbrush, and the cups of tea are only mine, and no one but me is sleeping on those sheets I just bought.

And though I believe he is innocent. I do.
I *think* I do –

When I'm not in front of him, I'll think, why am I *sad* looking at this fucking Bed Bath and Beyond coupon I taped to the fridge?

I say to Pam, 'You're my best friend, please don't *fire* me.'

What the fuck am I *doing*?!

But he didn't do it. I don't think.
But the truth still stands:

...
I am in love with a convicted murderer on Death Row…

And I *know* how it sounds.
And *I* would never.
And I *am*. So.

Who *am* I… I guess.

16: SOME THINGS I WILL NEVER TELL YOU

The song concludes as JACKIE *sits at the table across from* NICK.

NICK. It's not your visiting day.

JACKIE. You are going to have to tell me all of it. Everything.

Beat.

NICK. – *Everything?*

JACKIE. If I'm going to help get you out… I need the whole story. From the beginning.

Lights shift.

17: 'THE OTHER NICK'

NICK. Okay, well in that case, I'm gonna have to teach you how to jack a car.
In the seventies, vehicles didn't have locks on the steering column, so you could just stick a screwdriver into the key slot and literally turn on the ignition.
Like cars were *begging* to be stolen.
My friend Eddie and I used to steal Fords…

NICK's friend, EDDIE, appears. He's high as fuck.

EDDIE. Yo!

NICK. Yo! You gotta understand, this is Philly. Stealing cars ain't a crime, / it's culture!

EDDIE. It's culture!

NICK. We'd take 'em for a joyride, park 'em right where we found 'em.

EDDIE. It's not stealing.

NICK. We were fifteen. So, it was more about *driving*. *Until* –

EDDIE. I found a guy who'll give us two hundred bucks if we steal him a car.

NICK. *Two hundred dollars??* For a car?

EDDIE.... I know! / *Sweet*!

NICK. *Sweet!* Done!

EDDIE. Okay, now he wants a Pontiac.

NICK. Why would anyone want a Pontiac?

EDDIE. Why you question it, man?? Let's just get that car / – Philly style.

NICK. Philly style!
We rock up to Philly airport, and wait for what we called –

NICK *and* EDDIE. *Vicks!*

NICK. You know what a vick is? A vick is somebody who took their luggage, walked their family inside... and... never had a car when they came out.

EDDIE steals keys from an audience member.

EDDIE. Babyyyy!

NICK *and* EDDIE. *You just got vicked!*

NICK. We take that money, and buy drugs.

NICK *and* EDDIE (*repeating, like a rap*). We take that money, buy drugs!
Take that money, buy drugs!
Take that money, buy drugs!

NICK. STOP! STOP! FUCK!!... I'm not saying I was a great guy.

EDDIE. You weren't.

NICK. I was a teenager hooked on methamphetamine.
My favorite *vein* was right here.
I can still feel the hole in my arm, the burning, the taste of ethanol, and it's like –
– the one time I'm at a loss for words.
Then... the other me came out.
The one who wasn't weak.
The one who wasn't full of fear: of the dark, of the woods, of what's lurking there.
Once I was on drugs, my parents kicked me out.
So, I was homeless for most of that year.
Stole two cars in a row, driving around at night, on a binge.
(*Looks around, confused.*) *Eddie?*

OFFICER BENJAMIN WRIGHT *pulls* NICK *over.*

OFFICER BENJAMIN WRIGHT *attempts to communicate with* NICK, *but* NICK *isn't lucid enough.*

OFFICER BENJAMIN WRIGHT. Officer Benjamin Wright.
I need you to roll down the window, son.

NICK. *Son.*

OFFICER BENJAMIN WRIGHT. Roll down the –

As BENJAMIN *does the 'roll down the window' gesture,* NICK *starts giggling.*

NICK. *Son?*

OFFICER BENJAMIN WRIGHT. License and registration and roll down / the –

NICK (*almost to himself, humming/singing*). Okay, Pops. Pop-pop-pop-pop-pop – Ba-ba-pop-da-bap-ba-da-da-da-da –

OFFICER BENJAMIN WRIGHT. Excuse / me?

NICK. Look at *you* packing HEAT!

OFFICER BENJAMIN WRIGHT. GET OUT OF THE CAR!!

NICK (*laughing*). Mmmmm. I don't know how good THAT's gonna / go –

OFFICER BENJAMIN WRIGHT. You didn't stop for that light. Didn't you see the stop sign?
Get out of the FUCKING CAR!

NICK *panics, stands.*

OFFICER BENJAMIN WRIGHT *places a resisting hand on* NICK*'s shoulder, seizes* NICK*'s shirt front and pins* NICK *against the car, forearm to* NICK*'s throat.*

STAND STILL, STAND / STILL!!

NICK. What? What's happening?!

NICK *pushes* OFFICER BENJAMIN WRIGHT*'s hand away.*

OFFICER BENJAMIN WRIGHT *grabs his club from his belt, raising it to strike* NICK. NICK *looks up at the club and takes it with a swift yank, laughing.*

OFFICER BENJAMIN WRIGHT. What?

OFFICER BENJAMIN WRIGHT *takes his pistol from its holster.* NICK *grabs the* OFFICER*'s wrist, still confused and laughing.*

But then it turns dangerous. They are now in a fight for control of the gun.

They tussle back and forth, NICK *keeps trying to push the gun away.*

BANG. Suddenly, the gun goes off.

NICK. Okay, okay, let's / stop, stop, stop –

NICK *reaches to help* OFFICER WRIGHT *up.*

Here, here, here –

OFFICER BENJAMIN WRIGHT. You son of a bitch, almost got us killed!
Get in the car, ya big idiot!! The fuck am I supposed to call in.

NICK. And he shut me in back cage area. He didn't even seem scared, he just looked at me and smiled.

OFFICER BENJAMIN WRIGHT. Shots fired, officer assist.

NICK. I remember he said it four times.

OFFICER BENJAMIN WRIGHT. Shots fired, officer assist.

NICK. I was just sitting / there –

OFFICER BENJAMIN WRIGHT. Shots fired, officer assist.

NICK. What the hell just / happened?

OFFICER BENJAMIN WRIGHT. Shots fired, officer / assist.

18: WHAT ARE MY CHARGES?

NICK. They throw me in the intake unit and I crash.

JACKIE. You get a public defender?

NICK. Young kid.

JACKIE. Shit.

The PUBLIC DEFENDER *enters*.

PUBLIC DEFENDER. Mr Yarris, do you understand the serious nature of your charges?

NICK. Oh, God.

PUBLIC DEFENDER. Because if you are convicted, you face life imprisonment.

NICK. What are my charges?

PUBLIC DEFENDER. Reckless endangerment. Robbery, resisting arrest, possession of narcotics, possession of a stolen vehicle.

NICK. I mean – it's not ideal.

OFFICER BENJAMIN WRIGHT. *Kidnapping* of a police officer.

NICK. Kidnapping?!

OFFICER BENJAMIN WRIGHT. Attempted *murder* of a police / officer.

NICK. What?

OFFICER BENJAMIN WRIGHT *and the* PUBLIC DEFENDER *disperse*.

JACKIE. But wait, none of these would even get you the death penalty??

NICK (*to* JACKIE). So, I'm sitting in my cell, and there's this old-ass newspaper in there too, and the paper's like calling me. So, I pick it up and I read: *Delaware County Daily Times*. Headline: MOTHER LINDA MAE CRAIG FOUND SLAIN.

JACKIE. December 1981, Linda Mae Craig left work at the Tri-State Mall in Wilmington, Delaware. As she got into her car, she was punched in the face, breaking her teeth. She was then dragged out of her shoes, and stuffed into her trunk.

NICK. Man, I only lived about twenty miles from the murder scene.

JACKIE. She was driven three miles into the state of Pennsylvania, and stabbed in the chest six times after being raped. Her dying body was dumped in the snow in a church parking lot.

NICK. It was horrible to even read…
And I start thinking: If I had knowledge about a crime *this* big, I could get out of my charges.
I had the stupid mind of a child. A delusional, meth-head child.
So, I start making up a story. I *know* how to tell a story.
(*To the* PUBLIC DEFENDER.) I know who killed Linda Mae Craig.

PUBLIC DEFENDER. You do?

NICK *(to* JACKIE). – I didn't.
(*To* PUBLIC DEFENDER.) Of course I do! A tip like that should be worth something, right?

PUBLIC DEFENDER. *If* you know who did this, it's worth a hell of a lot.

NICK. Okay. Jimmy Brisbois did it!

PUBLIC DEFENDER. Who in the hell is Jimmy Brisbois?

NICK. Met Jimmy when we was doing drugs and selling jewelry that I found in a car I stole from the airport.

PUBLIC DEFENDER. Um, are you sure you want me to put all of that on your record?

NICK. It's fine, it's fine.
(*To* JACKIE.) It's perfect! I give 'em this guy *Jimmy Brisbois*, who I hate, who used to beat on me, who also happens to be dead. I heard he OD'd.
They'll go lookin' for *Jimmy*, and when they realize he's *dead*, nobody ends up in jail, nobody gets hurt, and I get out of here for a good tip! Houdini-style...

JACKIE. What?

NICK. I dunno, that's what I thought would work.

COP. Is that so?

NICK. Yeah, that's so. I'm telling you, officer. Jimmy Brisbois! He *bragged* about killing Mrs Craig.

COP. *If* this is true, this is going to go very well for you, Nick. Let's get the captain.

The COP *takes* NICK's *handcuffs off, as the* CAPTAIN *enters.*

CAPTAIN (*to* COP). Hey, go get this boy a drink, man.

NICK. You got like – Sprite?

COP. *Sprite?*

CAPTAIN. *Sprite?*

NICK. I don't know. Fruit punch?

CAPTAIN. What're you, seven years old?
   Get him a Diet Coke.
   That's what adults drink.

COP runs out to the theater lobby.

NICK. And some Doritos?

CAPTAIN (*shouting to Cop*). Nacho flavor! Get two!
   (*Back to* NICK.) You're a young guy.
   Orderin' Sprites.
   There's *a lot* going on in America right now, easy to get lost.
   In a city of violence, you're just one kid.
   So what's this bullshit, attempted murder of a cop?
   That doesn't sound like you, Nick. You're a car thief. What's going on?

NICK (*to* JACKIE). I tell him my story.
   How I was high, and resisted arrest, and the gun went off.
   How I'm happy to help with this Linda Mae Craig case.
   (*To* CAPTAIN.) How I know this drug addict named Jimmy who did it.

CAPTAIN. That's good, son. Real / good –

NICK (*to* JACKIE). Captain's like a proud parent.
   The *looks* he's giving me, the encouragement, the *snacks*.

COP returns from the theater lobby concession stand with chips and soda.

COP. No Doritos out there, just this. And the Diet Coke out there was seven bucks.

CAPTAIN. – for *soda*?! The fuck?!

They give NICK *the chips and soda, which he eats happily.*

NICK. S'good. Thank you.

CAPTAIN. Do you realize that in a few hours, you've gone from prison for the rest of your life… to your charges being reduced to just resisting arrest?

NICK. I do.
   (*To* JACKIE.) It's working, it's fucking working!! Until –

A knock on the door. COP *re-enters.*

COP. Jimmy Brisbois has got an airtight alibi. He's clean, sober, and innocent.

NICK. Wait, hold on, Jimmy Brisbois is alive?

CAPTAIN. Wait, hold on. You thought he was *dead*?

NICK. No, nope – hold on, never mind that!

JIMMY BRISBOIS *appears.*

JIMMY BRISBOIS. My brother's dead. *Joey.* Not *Jimmy.*

NICK. Joey, Jimmy. Everybody in Philly's got the same damn sounding name!

JIMMY BRISBOIS. Can I go? Baby got naptime.

NICK. Sorry, Jimmy.

JIMMY BRISBOIS *exits. Everyone turns to* NICK.

CAPTAIN. How come you know all about that murder, son?

NICK. There was a newspaper, / I –

COP. You been locked up the whole time, how you gettin' a / paper?

NICK. There was a paper in my cell!

CAPTAIN. How you know so much about this dead woman, Nick?

NICK (*to* JACKIE). They see I'm a twenty-year-old drug addict, sitting in jail for the attempted murder of a police officer.
They see no one will ever believe a word I say.
They see this whole story, they don't see me.

CAPTAIN. Mr Yarris, you are formally charged with the abduction, rape, and murder of / a woman–

NICK. – a woman I had never met in my life.

19: ALL RISE

NICK *stands with his* PUBLIC DEFENDER *in front of* JUDGE KELLY.

BAILIFF. All rise. Department One of the Superior Court is now in session, Judge Robert Kelly presiding.

JUDGE KELLY. Be seated. Mr Yarris, you are standing trial today for the attempted murder and kidnapping of Officer Benjamin Wright.

But before going on record, I just want to make sure I read this correctly? – since being in jail for that, your client has *also* been charged with the abduction, rape, and murder of a Linda Mae Craig?

PUBLIC DEFENDER. Yes, Your Honor.

JUDGE KELLY. Alright. Well, we will try your murder case separately, on a different day. Bring in the jury. The prosecution may call its first witness.

PROSECUTOR. The people call Officer Benjamin Wright to the stand.

NICK. – and this joker... I'm tellin' you, the officer basically *limps* up there.

OFFICER BENJAMIN WRIGHT (*melodramatically*). When I pulled up to the car, Mr Yarris sucker-PUNCHED me in the / jaw.

NICK. What?

OFFICER BENJAMIN WRIGHT. I'm flailing, while he *PUMMELS* me in the face, before STEALING my gun. Mr Yarris then points the gun DIRECTLY at my face – and alls I'm thinking of is my family. If only I could see my sweet lil baby Darlene again.

NICK. Jesus Christ. Give the guy an Oscar.

OFFICER BENJAMIN WRIGHT. And my mama who's got the diabetes!

NICK. Fuckin' Daniel Day Lewis over here.

OFFICER BENJAMIN WRIGHT. So, I *heroically* pull the gun away from him as it DISCHARGES right next to my face. My ears are still ringing.

PROSECUTOR. Officer Wright, could you please describe Exhibit A to the jury.

OFFICER BENJAMIN WRIGHT. These are photos of my very badly scratched-up hands. Very bad.

PROSECUTOR. I have no further questions for this witness, Your Honor.

JUDGE KELLY. Does the defense wish to cross-examine the witness?

PUBLIC DEFENDER. Yes, Your Honor.

OFFICER BENJAMIN WRIGHT. Into my good ear, please.

The PUBLIC DEFENDER *walks calmly to the stand.*

PUBLIC DEFENDER. Let me get this straight. Your testimony is that the defendant sucker-punched you, and then beat you with your seven-pound metal gun? I imagine that left a pretty good mark.

OFFICER BENJAMIN WRIGHT. Oh, absolutely it did.

PUBLIC DEFENDER. Why weren't photos of your face taken?

OFFICER BENJAMIN WRIGHT. I'm a good-looking man. And don't need the jury seein' my bruises... I got my pride.

PUBLIC DEFENDER. No further questions, Your Honor.

JUDGE KELLY *scoffs.*

JUDGE KELLY. – yeah, I mean that's about the craziest thing I ever heard in my court.
We will now stand in recess as we await the verdict. Officer Wright, if you go outside, I suggest you purchase sunscreen for your delicate features.

NICK. The jury was out only a *very* short time, came right back –

JUDGE KELLY. How do you find the defendant –

An envelope is handed to an audience member.

AUDIENCE MEMBER. Not guilty. On all charges.

NICK. Thank you! Freedom!
And my mom was there!

PROSECUTOR (*to the jury*). You just let a murderer go!

PUBLIC DEFENDER. Excuse me, we didn't try his murder case today. We tried this case, and your case stinks.

20: ANOTHER DAY IN COURT

JACKIE. You had the same prosecutor on your next case, didn't you?

NICK. Yeah. And after they lost –

PROSECUTOR. Yes, Your Honor, we are now seeking the death penalty.

PUBLIC DEFENDER. This isn't / a sentence hearing!

JUDGE KELLY (*turns to the jury*). Good afternoon, everyone. I thank you for sitting on today's jury – the Commonwealth of Pennsylvania versus Nicholas James Yarris who is charged with the first degree abduction, rape, and murder of Linda Mae Craig.
This is a capital case, so please give it your full attention as if it were *you* on trial, and your own life were at stake.
That said, I'm sure many of you are worried about making it to your barbecues this beautiful July Fourth holiday weekend, so we'll try to keep it quick, get you out before the town fireworks begin.

NICK (*to* JACKIE). He actually fucking said that.

JUDGE KELLY. Be seated.

PROSECUTOR. The prosecution calls to the stand, Arthur Craig, the victim's *husband*. First slide.

Click.

ARTHUR CRAIG. That's my – wife, Linda Mae. And our three adopted children. That's my family.

PROSECUTOR. Please, tell the jury about your wife?

ARTHUR CRAIG *speaks in one long run-on.*

ARTHUR CRAIG. Together since we was seventeen. *Years* we been happy, till they closed my mill, so I asked her to get a seasonal job, so our kids could still have Santa.

PUBLIC DEFENDER. Objection, Your Honor. Unfair, / prejudicial.

JUDGE KELLY. Overruled. Please continue, Mr Craig.

ARTHUR CRAIG. I keep thinkin' lately 'bout why things happen – Tuesday I'm hidin' her presents in the attic, Wednesday I'm a widower.

PUBLIC DEFENDER. Objection – irrelevant / evidence –

JUDGE KELLY. Overruled!

ARTHUR CRAIG. How was I to know when I gave her that clippin' for a job at the mall, that it would end with my Linda being *raped*, and cut out of her coat, stabbed *sixteen* times, and left to bleed in the snow by THAT man there!!

ARTHUR CRAIG *points at* NICK. *Everyone looks.*

PUBLIC DEFENDER. Objection!

NICK (*to* JACKIE)....Eyes.
 Eyes following his finger, pointing at me.
 The jury – looked at the pictures, then looked at me.
 Like in those nature documentaries where all the animals do an alike thing.
 And it was the last time, for the rest of the trial, they ever looked in my direction.

JUDGE KELLY. On the charge of first degree abduction, how do you find the defendant?

JURY FOREMAN. Guilty.

NICK. Mom!! MOM – Mom, / Mom, Mom –

JUDGE KELLY. Control your client, or I will hold him in contempt –   PUBLIC DEFENDER. Nick, *please* –

JUDGE KELLY. On the charge of first degree rape, how do you find the defendant?

JURY FOREMAN. Guilty.

NICK (*in a panic*). MOM!! NOOOO, MOM!! I DIDN'T DO IT!

JACKIE. Nick –   PUBLIC DEFENDER. Nick –

JUDGE KELLY. ORDER IN THE COURT!!!!!!
On the charge of murder in the first degree, how do you find the defendant?

JURY FOREMAN. Guilty.

JUDGE KELLY. On all charges, we find the defendant, guilty.

PUBLIC DEFENDER. I'm sorry.

Beat.

NICK (*to* JACKIE). They just needed someone to blame.

JACKIE. And there you were…

NICK. And the jury got out in time to go swimming and eat their hot dogs.

21: THE KEY TO MY CELL

The trial disappears and NICK *is just sitting at the table, talking to* JACKIE.

JACKIE. Wait. Okay. Wait. Was there any evidence presented at your murder trial?

NICK. No. Nothing.

JACKIE. There was *no* evidence presented against you?

NICK. No. No, none.

JACKIE. *Nothing* linking you to the crime scene?

NICK. How could there be?

JACKIE. But you – signed a confession?

NICK. No.

JACKIE. Eyewitness testimony?

NICK. No. Well, one woman said she saw me at the mall the day before.

JACKIE. Like there'd be no other six-foot white men at a mall in Delaware.
 Did they – ever find a murder weapon, / or –

NICK. No, / no.

JACKIE. Any evidence, any *evidence* at all?

NICK. I did share a blood type with the murderer. / But –

JACKIE. A blood type is meaningless. It ties you to *millions*, that's all.

NICK. That's all that was available. That's why I mailed you the article. 'Cause DNA is more specific, right?

JACKIE (*a laugh*). – *Yes*. Yes, it is.

NICK. Well, then I think all they gotta do is test it. 'Cause none of my biological material's anywhere near her. 'Cause *I* was *never* anywhere near her. Ever. I swear.

JACKIE. Nick, how have you never told anyone?

NICK. It takes a long time to tell my story.
No one listens.
All I'm guilty of was being a very dumb kid...

JACKIE.... Nick. *If* this is true, you would have the *key* to your cell.

JACKIE *rips off a piece of paper.*

Okay, okay, we need to get your lawyer here –

NICK. Joe Bullen, he's a fuckin' asshole.

JACKIE. He's still your lawyer. We'll ask him to petition the courts to gather the trial evidence from the autopsy, and test the DNA. You should write a letter to go with it. Should be straightforward, quick. Once they test it, you could be out of here by New Year's.

NICK. You think we could spend it together?

JACKIE. Just write your letter. I'll write one, too.
But – yeah, I always host.

NICK *writes.* JOE BULLEN *appears.*

JOE BULLEN. Alright, let's see what you've got.

JACKIE *and* NICK *in front of* JOE BULLEN:

JACKIE (*reading from her letter*). 'The first thing you should know is that this is true. It's what actually happened.
I know it seems like it's a story – inside of a story – inside of a story – but that's how it is for most people. At least the ones in here.'

JOE BULLEN *takes the letter.*

JOE BULLEN. This is *way* too long, but alright. I'll file your letters with the petition, and see if we can get the DNA tested. If this works, you'll be the first.

NICK. And now?

JOE BULLEN. We wait.

JACKIE. Okay! I'll wait. We'll wait.

NICK. We wait.

A series of phone calls. Another day. New Year's Eve.

PRE-RECORDED MESSAGE. Do you accept a collect call from the Department of Corrections, state of Pennsylvania?

JACKIE. Yes.
(*On the phone with* NICK.) I'm on pins and / needles.

NICK. I'm trying not to hope too much, / but –

JACKIE. Five, four, three, two, one! Happy New Year!

Another day. 4th of July.

PRE-RECORDED MESSAGE. Do you accept a collect call from the Department of Corrections, state of Pennsylvania?

JACKIE. I know July Fourth is probably hard for you. But hopefully it's your last one in there.

Another day. Halloween. Jackie's doorbell rings as she answers the phone.

(*Calling offstage.*) Mom, can you get the door?

ANNOUNCER. Do you accept a collect call / from the Department of Corrections, state of Pennsylvania?

JACKIE. Okay, I'll get it.

The sound of 'trick-or-treat!' at the door.

(*Into the phone.*) Yes.

Another day. Thanksgiving. NICK *looks at a picture* JACKIE *has sent.*

Happy Thanksgiving, baby!

NICK. Happy Thanksgiving.

The sound of two dogs barking in the background.

What was that?

JACKIE. That's *yours* –
 I wanted to surprise you. The little mutt ran in front of my car last week, so I scooped her up.
 Jocko Two, we'll call her. She'll be waiting for you when you get out.
 …
 … I believe you, Nick Yarris.

NICK. No one has *ever* said that to me – ever.

JACKIE. I believe / you.

Another day. Christmas Eve.

PRE-RECORDED MESSAGE. Do you accept a collect call from the Department / of –

NICK. Why haven't I heard from you, Mr Bullen?

JOE BULLEN. I got some news for you, Nick. / Sorry to have to give it to you on Christmas Eve.

NICK. What?
 Come on tell me, tell me, tell me, I can barely hear / you –

JOE BULLEN. You gotta calm down, / okay?

NICK. What? I am calm, / *what*?

JOE BULLEN. I just got off the phone with the coroner's / office and –

NICK. WHAT?
 – there's these – THEY JUST BROUGHT IN DINNER, THEY'RE BANGING THESE METAL TRAYS, I CAN'T / HEAR –

JOE BULLEN. They've – *lost* all the autopsy material.

NICK (*to* JOE BULLEN). Say that again, what do –
 (*Turning around into the noise.*) JUST SHUT UP, PLEASE!!!!
 (*Into the phone.*) What are you talking about? What do you mean they *lost* the autopsy materials?

JOE BULLEN. That would have been the quickest way to get DNA tested. But it's *gone*. We can try tracking down other evidence, but who knows how it's been stored or where.

NICK. Hold on. The evidence from my trial, is *missing*? Is that what you are trying to tell me?

JOE BULLEN. The coroner's office has been looking for the last year and a half. But they've *lost* the autopsy material for Linda Mae / Cr–

NICK. Do you understand what you are saying?
Do you understand what you are even saying to me?
Do you get it?
Do you know what it is that you have just fucking said?
Do you?
'Cause I don't think you do. If you're saying it to me like that, I don't think you do!!

JOE BULLEN. I need you to calm down. These things / happen.

NICK. You remember when you told me I was guilty due to all the overwhelming evidence, well where's all that fucking evidence when I want DNA, Joe? WHERE THE *FUCK* IS THE EVIDENCE?

JOE BULLEN. If you're mad, I won't stay on this / phone –

NICK. Mad? I am so mad I will hunt you down and cut your fucking head off. Then you'll actually have a murderer to represent! You hear me?

JOE BULLEN *hangs up.*

Did you hang up? I know you didn't hang up on me, Mr Bullen. I know you / didn't –

GUARD. HEY! QUIET BEFORE I FIX YOU!

Another day.

JACKIE. I think you should marry me.

NICK. What?

JACKIE. I heard, I heard what's happening.
It will make it easier for me to get access to your records and help.
I know, so romantic.
It's not done. We're not done. We're not done.

22: A WEDDING

The MEN *sing a song of hope and new beginnings as* JACKIE *and* NICK *line up for their wedding.*

NICK. Oh my god, you smell so good.

JACKIE. You're so tall.

NICK. I'm so in love with you right now.
I can't believe it's the first time we're in the same room.

JACKIE. Sixteen years to the day that you were sentenced to die… we are starting a new life.

NICK. Everything is *beautiful* / now.

JACKIE. At your trial, you said the killer had B-positive blood.

NICK. I notice the *rain* now. Who the fuck am I?

JACKIE. So, I figured someone must have tested the blood at some point –

NICK. – every little nuance in life is magical. You've turned me into an idiot.

JACKIE. So, I thought even if the coroner's office lost the materials, the lab must have had it.

JACKIE *hands* NICK *a letter.*

'Dear Mr Yarris,
You are correct. The lab has searched our files and we do have… two slide preparations with high-weight, visible DNA which we would be happy to have tested for you…'

NICK. Are you fucking kidding me?

JACKIE. You can get out, Nick. Took longer than we thought, but – in the grand scheme of our life, the last eighteen months – it'll be a blink.

NICK. You're a genius!

JACKIE. – Okay. They test this, and you'll leave.
We're in this together.

They both look to the GUARD.

NICK. Can I at least put the ring on her finger?

GUARD. Be quick.

NICK. I'm gonna take you to Big Ben, Bed Bath, and g'damn Beyond.

JACKIE. To beyond this.

They exchange rings.
They hold hands.
They <u>hold</u> hands.
They touch, for the very first time ever. They linger.
They grasp fingers and then palms and then wrists and then – the GUARD *interrupts the moment.*

NICK. I can't kiss the bride?

GUARD. No. Time's up –

JACKIE. I'll come next Sunday, / it's –

GUARD. I have to get you back to your cell.

NICK. Come ON. It's my   GUARD. Time's up.
  wedding –

NICK. I love / you –

JACKIE. I love you, I love you, I – This is only temporary.

  NICK *is taken away.*

  JACKIE, *alone, looks at her ring...*
  And suddenly grows self-conscious.

(*To the audience*.) ...This. Is only *temporary*.

Another day.

...What're you like at a restaurant?

NICK. What do you mean?

JACKIE. Do you share food? Do you look at the prices or the descriptions first?
It says a lot about a person, the way they order.

NICK. You mean, am I cheap? Listen, if I get outta here, you can have anything you want on the menu.

JACKIE *laughs*.

I just hope, in this life, I get to love you. Properly.
'Cause, I know I'd do a really good job of it.

JACKIE (*to the audience*).... *Who says that?*

GUARD. Time, Yarris!

The singing is replaced with the soft pelting of light summer rain.

JACKIE (*to the audience*). We wait for a response.

NICK....

JACKIE (*to the audience*). But that one year becomes two.
(*To* NICK.) Don't lose / hope.

NICK. *You* don't lose / hope –

JACKIE. I'm good! I'm good!

JOE BULLEN. This is actually typical. These things take time.

JACKIE. Becomes three. *Three* years.

NICK. My lawyer says this is actually *typical*, if you can believe that.

JACKIE. I found a place closer to the prison so I don't have to drive every weekend –

NICK. Are you sure?

JACKIE *hands over a picture*.

JACKIE. Only temporary. See? The apartment's cute. Over in Alexandria.

NICK. That's your mom?

JACKIE. She helped me move in. She's coming around to all this, I think...

NICK. I could put her down as a visitor? I'm good with moms.

JACKIE. Not a good idea. She'll come to our wedding, though. If / we –

NICK. *When.*

JACKIE. When we redo it.

NICK. When.

JACKIE. And we'll honeymoon all over the UK –

NICK. We're hanging in there, right? Jackie?

JOE BULLEN. These things take time.

JACKIE. *Four* years, though?

NICK. It's been FOUR. GODDAMN YEARS.

JACKIE. – became – *five* – five years.

NICK. – *Jackie?*

JACKIE *shows* NICK *pictures.*

JACKIE. This is me in front of the Globe. I wept just to stand there.

NICK. Look at your pretty dress.

JACKIE. Only 'cause I ate so many scones my pants wouldn't close.
I brought you back a suitcase of Wotsits and Curly Wurlys and Frazzles –

NICK. What? What *words* are you saying –

JACKIE. – everything in England is named something *completely* insane.

I tried writing to the warden asking permission to bring them in, but –
I'll keep them for you, I won't eat them, promise.

JACKIE *smiles*. NICK *stares at the photo for a long beat*.

NICK.... This is what you look like in the world?
I've never seen you in the sun...

Beat.

JACKIE. You think you would have looked at me? Out there...

NICK. You think *you* would have looked at *me*.

Beat.

You went without me.

JACKIE. We'll go back, it's not a big deal. There are worse things than me going to England twice. Don't lose / hope.

NICK. I am not losing hope –
But I *am* starting to lose it.

JACKIE (*to the audience*). Six years.

NICK. It's been six FUCKING YEARS waiting for the results –

JACKIE. How long can it *possibly* / take –

JOE BULLEN *enters*.

JOE BULLEN. The results are / finally here.

JACKIE. The results – the results, / baby!

NICK. Do you wanna open it or should / I?

JACKIE. I thought they'd *call*, didn't / you?

NICK. I can't even look at it.

JACKIE. Why didn't they / *call*?

NICK. I feel sick, you – you open it.

JACKIE *opens the letter, reads...*

What?

JACKIE. – Inconclusive.

NICK. What?

JACKIE. Results are – inconclusive.

NICK. That's it?

JACKIE. I don't know, I –

> NICK *takes the letter, reads it.*

NICK. What??

> JACKIE *and* NICK *turn to* JOE BULLEN.

JOE BULLEN. Inconclusive results due to degradation. Is what it says.

NICK. It was degraded because it took them *six years* to test!

JOE BULLEN. It's – it's not actually the end.
Because of the degraded DNA – which was out of your control – we can now request the court find the victim's clothes.

NICK. I can't even keep track of this shit anymore.

JOE BULLEN. *If* they can find it, they can do a fresh test, rather than what had been improperly stored.

JACKIE. And then / what?

NICK. And then *what*, / Joe?

JACKIE. And then / what?

Another day.

JOE BULLEN. The clothes were found in a clerk's office, at the courthouse! Cuttings were sent to Maryland for keeping until we get court approval to test it.

NICK. So, what does that mean?

JOE BULLEN. We wait again.

JACKIE. We wait again.

NICK. Again?

JOE BULLEN. We need to beg the court to test.

Long beat.

NICK. How long?

JACKIE (*to the audience*). We wait another two years.

NICK. Two more *years* / of –

JACKIE (*to* NICK). Driving back and forth to the prison. Two more years of checking the mail, of watching my friends get married, have kids, or move to fellowships, new states, and start whole lives, while you and / I –

NICK. I don't know *how* you're still here.

JACKIE. I don't like when you say that.

NICK. It's *astonishing* you're still here –

JACKIE. I don't need that judgement from you, too.
(*To the audience*.) But the longer we wait, the more overwhelmed I am by time itself.
All those *years* wasted if I left... keep me here even longer – investing even more time I'll never get back.

JOE BULLEN. They're ready to test it. It's good. This is good news.
They've selected Doctor Blake, who did OJ's case.
They're sending the evidence to him in California as we speak.

A sudden shift.

Rain outside.

JACKIE *stands in front of* NICK, *soaking wet, speechless.*

JACKIE. I drove straight here. It's pouring out, / it's –

NICK. What? What happened?

JACKIE. They finally sent the evidence to California.

NICK. Yeah. And?

JACKIE. I don't know how I'm gonna –
I.
I can't – I can't say it.

NICK. What?

JACKIE. ...the – the package burst open in the mail.

NICK. ...what?

JACKIE. They – improperly packaged it – and it burst open, in transit.

NICK. ...what?

JACKIE. I don't know.

NICK. – what –

JACKIE. Doctor Blake won't test it. All it will do is produce results that the prosecution would contest, because of contamination.

NICK. I.
The.
– *what*.

JACKIE. In order for it not to be contested in the court, the *judge* or the prosecution would be the ones who would have to request testing –

NICK. Well, why the hell would they do that??

JACKIE. I don't know. But we – you – you *can't* anymore. There's – nothing more we can file, Nick.

Beat.

NICK. That's it?

JACKIE. It's done.

NICK. It's done? I'm goin' to the electric chair because – because of fucking FedEx?!

JACKIE. I don't –

NICK. Well. What are they doing with the rest of the evidence?

JACKIE. It's going back on a shelf.
And that's that...

NICK. This can't be real. This can't be real.
Real life.
– can it?

JACKIE. We're out of attempts. They're saying the decision is final.

Silence.

NICK. Can you say something?

JACKIE....

NICK. Can you *say* –

JACKIE. I don't –

NICK....

JACKIE....

NICK. It's going to be okay, right, / we'll –

JACKIE. – but / there's –

NICK. – there's got to be –

JACKIE....

NICK. *Something.*
Right?

JACKIE. I don't think so –

NICK. *Something.*

Beat.

JACKIE. *Nine. Years.*
Nine years we've been fighting to get the DNA.

NICK. What're you gonna do?

JACKIE. This – moment is not about me.

NICK. It is...

JACKIE. In nine years, the things I thought were temporary have become *permanent*, Nick...
I'm so far in, that when I walk the dog I think, 'that was a good walk,' but I no longer think about all the other places

I could be.
In nine years, the puppy I got us is an old dog.
I don't even mention her anymore, 'cause it just seems *mean*.
I haven't hosted New Year's since – I go out to eat, and I just stare at the menu, lost.
I think I'm – maybe losing the bits of myself that I liked?
I had wanted to be a mother. I just thought that was something I'd *do* one day –
I – I – I don't know what / to –

NICK. I think you do.

JACKIE. I *don't*.

NICK. Hey, you been locked up with me since I first quoted *Catcher in the Rye*.

Beat.

JACKIE (*with a smile*). – was that a move?

NICK. Oh, yeah. A *smooth* move.

JACKIE. A smooth move.

NICK. *Smooth* move.

JACKIE *laughs*.

It's okay to say it.

JACKIE. I. Can't do this anymore.

NICK. ... Good for / you.

JACKIE. Stop.

NICK. To say, 'I object' – to your own life...? Wish I'd done it myself – thirty years ago.

JACKIE. I'll still *call*, / and –

NICK. No, you don't have to call lawyers, or make copies of legal documents – you don't have to fight for me anymore. Be – *free*.
... One of us should be.

Beat.

JACKIE. I don't know what to do next.
  ... I'll always –

NICK. I know.

JACKIE. *Always*. I wish I / could –

GUARD. No touching.

NICK. I –

GUARD. No / touching.

JACKIE. I / didn't –

GUARD. What did I just / say?!

JACKIE. I still believe / you.

GUARD. Chrissakes, no touching! That's it, time's / up –

JACKIE. No, / please –

NICK. It's okay –
  It's okay. Go.
  Go.

  JACKIE *takes a breath. Gets up, walks out, down the long prison corridor.* NICK *watches her go.*

  She leaves, out into the Pennsylvania winter...

I watch Jackie walk out.
I feel – proud to get to watch her leave.
It's *strange* to feel *good* for her leaving, 'cause I know I've stolen so much of her life away...
She – was just this – *gift*.
She gave me my voice back. That voice that died – long before I lied about Linda Mae Craig, before I was boosting cars, before I was kicked outta my house. Way back.
The voice that died that day in the woods...
I take everything off the wall – put up just one picture – me as a kid with my dog.
I can't even look at it at first – but I try to start speaking politely to this tiny person.
Knowing *he* is the only one left.

  NICK *talks over the low hum of the singing.*

23: 'THAT WASN'T GOING TO BE MY LIFE'

NICK *sits center-stage in stoic silence.*

NICK. Few more years go by...

MAN 2. Inmate Nicholas Yarris has been on Death Row for nearly half his life.

NICK. *Time...* can be a blisteringly fast thing, where in the blink of an eye – ten years are gone from your life, but the next week is agony.

MAN 3. Death Row inmate Nicholas Yarris appears withdrawn.

NICK. Jackie doesn't visit again.
She writes to tell me our dog died of old age.
She says it was hard, at first, to forget me... until she filled her life up with other things.
Like a house in Seattle, a professor husband named *Ed*, and a baby boy.
She manages not to think about me anymore – except when a Bed Bath and Beyond coupon arrives and reminds her of how her life could have forked off in a completely different direction... but didn't.

MAN 6. Death Row inmate Nicholas Yarris is no longer getting out of bed.

NICK. I tear off her return address from her one letter.
I know I'll never go, but I can't throw it away.

MAN 4. Death Row inmate Nicholas Yarris is down nearly thirty-one pounds since his last weigh-in.

NICK. My younger brother, Marty, ODs in my parents' basement.
I can't go to his funeral, but I barely know him at this point.
I can't take the waiting around.
I'm just done.
So, I do what I've prepared myself to do – over the many years I've been in here.
I write...

Lights shift. NICK *writes a letter.*

Dear Judge Giles,
As a criminal defendant, I ask that the one right I have remaining to me be recognized.
And that is a condemned man's right to be executed.
I hereby withdraw all my appeals.
I request nothing for my last meal, but I do request my last words – as I intend to speak on my own behalf.
You see – on Death Row, I took up reading, to hear other stories, other voices.
Not just my own, replaying my mistakes, again and again.
Perhaps there was a moment you turned a corner, and everything could have been different.
There is such a small distance between having a life or... having it taken from you.
For the record, I maintain my innocence, but I am ready for my execution.
I forgive you for killing me.
I apologize for embarrassing my family.
And I accept my fate.
I hereby request counsel be dismissed, and Governor Rendell issue my execution date within sixty days of receipt of this letter.
Signed sincerely,
Nicholas James Yarris (Inmate AM 6841)

24: GET THE LAWYERS

JUDGE GILES *reads the letter.*

JUDGE GILES. Get the lawyers for a status conference, now. Mr Bullen. I would like to know why your client Nicholas Yarris – someone who has been *asking* for DNA testing for the last fifteen years, claiming they're innocent – is now writing to be executed...?

JOE BULLEN. He's what? – Lemme see –

JOE BULLEN *reads the letter. A* CLERK *enters*.

CLERK. Lunch!

The CLERK *hurries in with sandwiches.*

JUDGE GILES. What do we have, roast beef, / today?

CLERK. I got your gravy, I got your / provolone –

JUDGE GILES. Good, good.

JOE BULLEN (*re: the letter*).... Well, he's dismissed me, so I'm not sure what I can do.

JUDGE GILES. By law, I am required to transmit Mr Yarris's record to the governor, and law will require Mr Yarris be executed within sixty days of today. But something is not right to receive a letter like this. Whatever evidence remains, have DNA testing done immediately.

JOE BULLEN. *You're* requesting it?

JUDGE GILES. Now.

JOE BULLEN. That was the only way this was ever going to be allowed to happen again.

JUDGE GILES. With the highest priority.

Abrupt light shift.

GUARD. Yarris. Get up. Your lawyer is here to see you.

NICK *does nothing*.

Yarris. UP. NOW.

NICK *does nothing. The* GUARD *basically drags him up*.

AM 6841, UP, UP NOW!

JOE BULLEN *appears*.

JOE BULLEN. They did the testing, Nick.
The gloves that were left inside the victim's vehicle... were found to have DNA. DNA from Mrs Craig. And DNA from an unknown male. Not you.

A loud humming from the PRISON CHOIR, *blocking out everything* JOE BULLEN *is saying.*

NICK. ...

JOE BULLEN. Nick, are you with me?

NICK. ...

JOE BULLEN. There is no DNA from you whatsoever. You are innocent. Indisputable.

NICK. ...

JOE BULLEN. It actually *was* that simple.
 I guess, just took a while...
 I'm heading right now to file a motion with the court for your release.
 May take a few more months. But we're starting today.

NICK *sits on his bed and eventually curls into the fetal position.* GUARD *enters.*

GUARD. Yarris.

NICK *flinches.*

 Uh. Mr Yarris. Nick. I was just informed what's happening with you.
 Um. I don't know. Why don't you go on and have a shower, alright?

NICK. I get up.
 I put on my shower shoes.
 Guard grabs my arm gently, leaves me there under the cool water.
 So I can feel something.
 And I cry.
 I *cry* like you wouldn't believe.
 I waited *years* to cry like that.
 Maybe I'd been waiting to cry like that since the beginning.

NICK *takes his childhood photo off the wall, looks at it.*

25: THE BEGINNING

NICK *sits in the pouring shower which turns to pouring rain, bringing* NICK *back to his childhood.*

The hollow, drumming sound of rain falling.

NICK. When I was a kid we lived in a house with a fiberglass awning, and when it rained, it gave off this hollow, drumming sound.
I'd get Jocko, and we'd sit outside, under this tattered green blanket.
And we'd listen to the rain, and play out all these daydreams in my head, of all the adventures we'd have, all the different things I could do, all the different people I could be. And it was like this cocoon.
And the rain was like calling me.

And then it starts to rain inside the theater. The memory of rain and the shower intertwining.

NICK *edges forward towards the water... And then he stops.* NICK *doesn't want to go into the rain and the shower. Something is holding him back.*

So, I grab Jocko, and my bike. And I'm riding, and Jocko's running after me, and we go deeper and deeper into the woods. And that's when I see him.

An OLDER MAN, *faceless, wearing a hooded raincoat, stands in front of him. Out in the rain.*

Hobnail boots, denim jeans, white T-shirt, armband rolled up with a pack of Lucky's.

OLDER MAN. You want a cigarette, kid?

Everything the OLDER MAN *says hangs in the air for an uncomfortably long period of time.*

NICK.... no.

OLDER MAN. Why?

NICK. I'm not allowed.

OLDER MAN. What're you, ten?

NICK. Nine.
 I'm almost ten, but I'm not allowed to smoke so no, no thank you, sir.

OLDER MAN. You want it, don't you?

NICK. I –
 I looked up towards my house.
 It was so far away.

 NICK *looks up and looks at the* OLDER MAN.

 It's pouring onstage, onto NICK.

OLDER MAN. Hold it.
 Put your lips around it.
 Now puff.

NICK. I feel myself… drift away from myself.

OLDER MAN. Just put it in your mouth.
 …
 Now my turn, okay?

NICK. I feel this sound – the rock in his hand he hit me with.
 My head / goes –

OLDER MAN. Nice and / slow.

NICK. Blood's pouring down / my –

OLDER MAN. Nice and slow.

More rain.

NICK MOM!!!! MOM!!!!!!
Man's holding me down, I'm looking through the trees for Jocko –
Man bends, he's moaning kind of, but I'm – *gone*.

Beat.

OLDER MAN. When your mom asks if you had a good bike ride today, what'll you tell her?

NICK. I don't wanna lie.

OLDER MAN. – not lying.
It's telling stories.
Tell everybody you fell off a wall, that's how your pants got bloody.
You be a good storyteller, okay?

NICK. How long do I have to tell this story?

OLDER MAN. For as long as it takes...

NICK. And what if they find out the truth??

The OLDER MAN *disappears into the woods.*

Jocko!! Where are you??

NICK'S FATHER. Nick?

NICK. Dad?

NICK'S FATHER. Where'd Jocko go? Why'd you stop riding your bike and smiling, son?

NICK (*to* NICK'S FATHER). I fell, Dad, I fell...

(*To the audience.*) As soon as I'd told my story – to my dad, to the captain, Jimmy fucking Brisbois, it was like, once lies are believed, they're so hard to undo.
And then –
And then –

26: AND THEN FREEDOM

Coming out of the rain, out of the shower, out of the water, gently. GUARD *hands* NICK *a towel.*

GUARD. I left your towel on the radiator. My wife, Charlotte, bought me one of those towel heaters, but this works as well.

NICK. What?

GUARD. Just saying I – made sure your towel's nice and warm for you, Nick. Don't know what I can do – for you right now – other than that.

Throughout, NICK *dries himself off.*

NICK. I'm in my cell, waiting for them to process my final paperwork.
The guard has this little radio and I swear to God, playing Seal's 'Love's Divine'.
You couldn't get *away* from that song that summer – and –

The beautiful voice of WESLEY *comes back in, singing Seal's 'Love's Divine'. Soulful. Sincere. Maybe even this time* WESLEY *has a guitar, or* JACKIE *plays the violin from some place far away; something to differentiate from the other singing.*

That fuckin' song.
I pack a few of my belongings, my books, Jackie's address.

WESLEY *continues to sing.*

I walk out of prison, take a –
(*Hailing a cab.*) Taxi! Philly airport.
Book a one-way ticket to Seattle, buy a dozen roses when I land.
The cellophane wrapper keeps sticking to my sweaty palms as I pull up outside Jackie's house.

WESLEY *sings.*

Behind NICK, JACKIE *appears in her home.*

There it is.
The yellow door I saw on the library computer.

I see someone inside. It's *her.* It's actually her.
Jackie, after all these years.
She spots me through the window, drops the pot she's holding, rushes to the front porch.
I run up the lawn, take her face in my hands – and I, just *look* at her.
To see if she's still the person I knew, or if that world between us died and that dying makes her now a stranger.
I hold her as close as I can –
And –
And –

WESLEY *sings*.

And that's as far as I get when I picture it.
There is no good outcome if I go.

...

If she still feels the same way, it'll break her heart... and if she doesn't... it'll break mine.
I promise myself I must *never*, *ever* go to Seattle. I can never steal her freedom again.
I tear up her address, kiss the scraps, leave them behind.
And years from now, when I tell my story, I'll change some details about Jackie.
Keep the truth the same, but protect her a little.
She's got her new beginning. And I've got mine.

GUARD. Nick. Right this / way –

NICK. I stand –
They open my / cell.

GUARD. Nick. Come / on.

NICK. I see my hands and they're not cuffed this time...
They're not cuffed – (!!) And the other inmates come to the front of their cells. Hardened murderers *clapping*, weeping.
As if they're getting some kind of justice for themselves.

GUARD. Right here – your / signature –

NICK. I'm signing, but I'm barely in that room, I'm just trying to –

GUARD. QUIET! And here, too.

NICK. – remember what it'll be like to feel free.

27: A NEW STORY

The stage crew clears everything away... They mop up the water until the stage is empty, clean.
The OTHER MEN *are gone. The stage crew goes.* WESLEY *is the last to leave.*

NICK *is alone onstage.*

NICK. I hadn't felt free since I was a runaway fugitive – that time I made it to New York.

   NICK *walks downstage, closer to the audience. Maybe even the house lights come up a little so he can talk directly to them.*

Back when I boosted a bicycle.
I hadn't been on a bike since I was a kid.
After that day in the woods, I couldn't even look at one. But *cycling*.
Well... it's kinda like riding a bike.

So, there I was, pedaling.
And I ride uptown, hitting the lights right, and I go, go, go.

It was one of the first days of spring. And it was like the sunshine had unlocked the whole city. Everywhere, people were comin' out of their apartments, realizing they could breathe again.
People *everywhere*, each with their own little stories.
And there I am with mine, right in the center of all possibility.
There's all the people I was, and the people I will never get to be, but there's also still hot-dog carts, and car horns, and girls who look like they're named Tiffany who I want to take for a drink.

And I think: I am *incredulous*.
I am *incredulous* that the world can still be this... wonderful.

And of course, of course, I know it isn't really.
As does every person laid out on blankets, trying to catch a ray of sun.
Of course I know my life – when I walk out those doors will be hard.
But that first day of spring??
Those first steps outside??
After so long.
After so. Long.
After so, so long.
To see that –
The skies are still blue...? The sun still shines...?
That I can still just – go buy an overpriced coffee. Pet a dog. And ride a bike...
That it's all still there.

– makes you kind of understand how some people believe in God.

And outta nowhere, the air starts to get heavy, like maybe rain.
And, of course, no one, *no one* thought to bring an umbrella.
'Cause for this one moment, this one day, they don't wanna believe it.
All these funny people in their stupid shorts, convinced the sun'll never end.

And the trees start shaking in the breeze, and people come out on their tiny balconies, and stop eating pizza, and the whole city takes a deep breath...

We all stand on that precipice.

We look up at the sky together...

hoping the rain will never come... and –

And –

But before NICK *can finish, a dog runs onstage.* NICK *is surprised to see this dog here. In front of him. In this theater of all places.*

NICK bends to pet the dog... His dog licks his face. NICK is innocent again, almost childlike. NICK and his dog leave the theater together, heading out into the real world as it unfurls before them, with all its unlikely possibilities.

End of play.

Afterword:
A Letter from Nick Yarris

Hello.

My name is Nicholas James Yarris. As I share these words with you about this play, which has been adapted from the film documentary entitled *The Fear of 13,* I am 63 years of age… which I assure you, I never thought I would live to be.

I have never shared any of this with anyone before now, and yet it now seems appropriate to do so here…

I appreciate how many of us are in wonder about how much time we have to be alive on this earth; how long we have to share our unique experiences of what life has meant to us, as we all try valiantly to find meaning in what we encounter.

During the making of the documentary in 2007, I was tasked with a very complex opportunity to use my accumulated efforts of being an autodidact, self-educated man to sit before a camera and bring my own story to life.

Living inside of a solitary confinement cell for either 22, 23 or 24 hours of each day over the course of 23 years has allowed me precious few gifts. However, one of the best gifts I own now is that I have memory recall driven into me from what is known as 'No new sensory input.' On Death Row, each day is the same routine, each day the same world is the blank wall of your cell. It is in this manner that you are stripped of new memory-making, leaving you only with your yesterdays to think about. I loathed the many negative memories which I feared would never stop hurting to think of, while I adored the ones that made me feel a tiny bit of worth.

To do this story justice, I felt I had to ask the documentary team only one thing for my efforts: to build me a prison cell so that I could, one last time, go back to a world I knew, to share my memory of what unfolded.

This faux cell that David Sington created for me in Ealing Studios gave me the courage to go back to 'Death Row' in the way I needed, and in my way of having spoken to myself for many years, I told my story in depth and fairness.

When I finished filming with David, I was no longer afraid to die. I had experienced something few men live to tell of – and trauma that should have crushed me mentally before then. I had no clue that I was going to be given such a magnificent gift to appreciate all my days, but that is really what I needed.

My lone fear I had when I was given back my freedom in 2004 was if I would die before I could tell my story in full. It is the absolute truth that each of us must experience life first, and then in whatever aftermath of those events, it can be shared as a memory to others. The ones who read this who are carrying serious trauma like I have gone through know exactly what I mean. I wish someone hears you fully one day, and I pray to God that moment validates you for your life. I have been shown how important it is for someone to tell me, 'Thank you for loving me', and I have offered, 'Thank you for letting me love you.' Just having someone be thanked for their love gives them so much, just hearing this in return has made me believe in everything good about myself.

That is where this play, created by Lindsey Ferrentino, gets its origins. We are all searching for the ability to find within ourselves a beauty or strength that will be our defining memory in times of trouble or sorrow. We want so much to be the ones who persevere, rise, and set examples. I am so humbled to be a small part of this overall good we seek as humans.

I went from seething anger that was so replete with ugliness that I would literally sit in my cell and beat the back of my head against the wall. I did so because I believed I was so ruined as a human that my only hope for survival was with the help of my anger. I am ashamed that I allowed myself to feel so worthless for so long. And yet, without even knowing it, I clung to what makes each of us human and I used this as my only retort to living in the gallows of America.

How I got to think in such a way emerged from a series of events:

In July of 1982, the Delaware County courthouse was struck by lightning during my trial for the rape and murder of a woman whom I had never met in my life. The jury had just been shown projected slides on a portable screen of the victim lying dead on the frozen earth.

That evening, in the basement of the courthouse, as my trial attorney stuck his arms through the bars of my cell and cried uncontrollably, I stood and comforted him. At age 21, sentenced to die twenty minutes before then, it should have been me crying with my arms outstretched, seeking comfort and needing someone to hold me through such a terrible ordeal. Instead, I saw how my life was touched by God, and with a knowing that I had not killed anyone in my life, surely this was a journey that I was on, and not my doom. In no way could I have predicted how I would regain freedom. That series of events is as profound to me as a bolt of lightning stopping my trial.

For so many of us, we feel we are forced to live a certain way because where we live makes us *have* to be this way. I decided no. I did not care what the consequences were, I stopped being led by fear, or another's notion of who I was. I decided that what was taught to me by my parents meant more to me than the vulgarity I was being shown by others. When I was told I was nothing, that I deserved the worst treatment; when I looked at what was done to me with clubs, fists and boots, I saw how much I needed to give myself love and give love to others.

I helped men in prison with scrambled minds by writing letters to their attorneys, loved ones, and filling out forms for them to acquire new bedding, or small, regulated items. In time, I learned to be as human as possible while living in hell. This simple act of holding on to what I considered precious is the one thing that made me not like all the others around me. I became alive inside while I was locked up in a maximum-security unit, waiting to be murdered by the state. I went from being nothing but lost in my own anger and self-abuse to singing, sharing what good I had, and making myself feel as if I had a duty to hold onto my wit with laughter.

They say only madmen laugh in the gallows. Only the ones devoid of reality or care laugh openly while on Death Row. My laughter was not born of such ignorance. I had achieved something truly unique. I had come to find within me a desire to be alive that was so brilliant it became a gift others wanted to know.

On 16 January 2004, I was uniquely born to this world a second time. I did not exist in computer files, nor did I have any history as an adult outside of prison. Not one single certificate of education, no training, or work qualifications. I started off with zero chance to make much of myself. Released to live in my elderly parents' home in Philadelphia, I had two real choices before me: I could believe those things that made me feel alive in my cell on Death Row, or I could be bitter about it all and beat my head on a wall in anguish. I chose right then to use the education I had given myself to transform the projected path of my own life.

I went from living in the basement of my parents' home with nothing, to continuing this journey across the world. In the twenty years I have been free, there are literally thousands of others who have shared with me how my story has saved their lives. My efforts to hold on to my humanity allowed them to keep their sanity and hope in life. I feel a great sense of humility and gratitude for how my efforts have been a balm of relief to someone else; to have taken all that I experienced and used it as a cathartic healing for myself, as well as for those I am allowed to love or meet in life. It is somehow like I was made to know the worst reflections of faces while they looked at me and thought my hands were red with murder, to having the eyes of angels know me for the good that I have brought to their lives. My only real achievements in life are that I somehow managed to go to Death Row for decades as an innocent man, and then come back with my humanity not only intact, but made brighter for it all.

I am finally outwardly boyishly happy. Joyous and alive like I deserve to be. I have love, care and consideration. I am filled with hope that this play will bring my story to life so beautifully... that it will offer me the dream I have to finally heal.

I am so grateful that this play is an examination of what we all can be in life, that love and understanding can save us from feeling unappreciated or empty. The most profound feeling I am left to share is how I am now part of our cultural history. Long after I am gone, someone will witness my life, and I will never know them. I can never truly die now, as I am forever part of our world's art.

I want folks to know how lucky I feel to have been alive on Death Row and survived; how lucky I am to be alive to this point where I am seeing the pay-off. I vow to be worthy of your consideration and respect, while I thank you so kindly for validating me with your love and acceptance.

To my daughter Lara Rebecca, I share the following...

Life is more than merely being alive. My darling child, it is in the finest moments of pain, or glory that we are able to really see who we are to our own self. I pray that you find your best qualities in each scenario. I am so honored to be part of your own story and journey, one that I know you will share in both depth and honesty, as I have done. Your grandmother Harriet Jayne Yarris had a saying that goes, 'The world is full of people, yet there are only so many human beings. When you find them, you love *them*, because they are the ones who do all the good for the world.'

I know you will choose wisely, and your good will be as meaningful one day as mine is now to the millions of human beings all over the world who love your daddy for all that he is as a man.

With love always,
Nick Yarris

www.nickhernbooks.co.uk

facebook.com/nickhernbooks

twitter.com/nickhernbooks